THE EGO
AND THE ID

By SIGMUND FREUD

AN AUTOBIOGRAPHICAL STUDY

BEYOND THE PLEASURE PRINCIPLE

CIVILIZATION AND ITS DISCONTENTS

THE COMPLETE INTRODUCTORY LECTURES ON PSYCHOANALYSIS

THE EGO AND THE ID

FIVE LECTURES ON PSYCHOANALYSIS

THE FUTURE OF AN ILLUSION

GROUP PSYCHOLOGY AND THE ANALYSIS OF THE EGO

INHIBITIONS, SYMPTOMS AND ANXIETY

INTRODUCTORY LECTURES ON PSYCHOANALYSIS

JOKES AND THEIR RELATION TO THE UNCONSCIOUS

LEONARDO DA VINCI AND A MEMORY OF HIS CHILDHOOD

NEW INTRODUCTORY LECTURES ON PSYCHOANALYSIS

ON DREAMS

ON THE HISTORY OF THE PSYCHOANALYTIC MOVEMENT

AN OUTLINE OF PSYCHOANALYSIS

THE PSYCHOPATHOLOGY OF EVERYDAY LIFE

THE QUESTION OF LAY ANALYSIS

TOTEM AND TABOO

THE STANDARD EDITION

OF THE COMPLETE PSYCHOLOGICAL WORKS OF

SIGMUND FREUD

24 VOLUMES

Sigmund Freud

THE EGO
AND THE ID

TRANSLATED BY

Joan Riviere

REVISED AND EDITED BY

James Strachey

WITH A BIOGRAPHICAL
INTRODUCTION BY

Peter Gay

W·W·NORTON & COMPANY

New York · London

ISBN 0-393-00142-3

W. W. Norton & Company, Inc., is also the publisher of The Standard Edition of the Complete Psychological Works of Sigmund Freud.

W. W. Norton & Company, Inc., 500 Fifth Avenue
New York, N.Y. 10110
W. W. Norton & Company Ltd. 10 Coptic Street
London WC1A 1PU

PRINTED IN THE UNITED STATES OF AMERICA

1 2 3 4 5 6 7 8 9 0

EDITORIAL NOTE

Since the original publication of the English translations of Freud's works there has been appearing the new authoritative text of *The Standard Edition of the Complete Psychological Works of Sigmund Freud,* translated from the German under the general editorship of James Strachey, in collaboration with Anna Freud, assisted by Alix Strachey and Alan Tyson. The Institute of Psycho-Analysis therefore thought it would be desirable to use this new text when reprinting the International Psycho-Analytical Library edition as the stocks of these began to get low. With the generous co-operation of Mr. Strachey and his collaborators and of the Hogarth Press this aim has been achieved, and in future as it becomes necessary to reprint any of Freud's works they will appear in a new edition in the International Psycho-Analytical Library with the text of *The Standard Edition.*

The present edition of Freud's *The Ego and the Id* contains the completely revised and fully annotated text of *The Standard Edition.* A bibliography and index have been provided and the volume has been prepared for publication by Angela Richards.

It is the hope of the Publications Committee that these revised texts with their annotations will be useful to the growing number of students of psycho-analysis.

J. D. Sutherland
*General Editor of The
International Psycho-Analytical
Library*

Contents

SIGMUND FREUD: A BRIEF LIFE
by Peter Gay

It was Freud's fate, as he observed not without pride, to "agitate the sleep of mankind." Half a century after his death, it seems clear that he succeeded far better than he expected, though in ways he would not have appreciated. It is commonplace but true that we all speak Freud now, correctly or not. We casually refer to oedipal conflicts and sibling rivalry, narcissism and Freudian slips. But before we can speak that way with authority, we must read his writings attentively. They repay reading, with dividends.

Sigmund Freud was born on May 6, 1856, in the small Moravian town of Freiberg.[1] His father, Jacob Freud, was an impecunious merchant; his mother, Amalia, was handsome, self-assertive, and young—twenty years her husband's junior and his third wife. Jacob Freud had two sons from his first marriage who were about Amalia Freud's age and lived nearby. One of these half brothers had a son, John, who, though Sigmund Freud's nephew, was older than his uncle.

---

[1] His given names were Sigismund Schlomo, but he never used his middle name and, after experimenting with the shorter form for some time, definitively adopted the first name Sigmund—on occasion relapsing into the original formulation—in the early 1870s, when he was a medical student at the University of Vienna. Freiberg, now in Czechoslovakia, bears the Czech name "Pribor."

Freud's family constellation, then, was intricate enough to puzzle the clever and inquisitive youngster. Inquisitiveness, the natural endowment of children, was particularly marked in him. Life would provide ample opportunity to satisfy it.

In 1860, when Freud was almost four, he moved with his family to Vienna, then a magnet for many immigrants. This was the opening phase of the Hapsburg Empire's liberal era. Jews, only recently freed from onerous taxes and humiliating restrictions on their property rights, professional choices, and religious practices, could realistically harbor hopes for economic advancement, political participation, and a measure of social acceptance. This was the time, Freud recalled, when "every industrious Jewish school boy carried a Cabinet Minister's portfolio in his satchel."[2] The young Freud was encouraged to cultivate high ambitions. As his mother's first-born and a family favorite, he secured, once his family could afford it, a room of his own. He showed marked gifts from his first school days, and in his secondary school, or Gymnasium, he was first in his class year after year.

In 1873, at seventeen, Freud entered the University of Vienna. He had planned to study law, but, driven on by what he called his "greed for knowledge," instead matriculated in the faculty of medicine, intending to embark, not on a conventional career as a physician, but on philosophical-scientific investigations that might solve some of the great riddles that fascinated him. He found his work in physiology and neurology so absorbing that he did not take his degree until 1881.

A brilliant researcher, he cultivated the habit of close observation and the congenial stance of scientific skepticism. He was privileged to work under professors with international reputations, almost all German imports and tough-

---

[2] *The Interpretation of Dreams* (1900), *SE* IV, 193.

minded positivists who disdained metaphysical speculations about, let alone pious explanations of, natural phenomena. Even after Freud modified their theories of the mind—in essence barely disguised physiological theories—he recalled his teachers with unfeigned gratitude. The most memorable of them, Ernst Brücke, an illustrious physiologist and a civilized but exacting taskmaster, confirmed Freud's bent as an unbeliever. Freud had grown up with no religious instruction at home, came to Vienna University as an atheist, and left it as an atheist—with persuasive scientific arguments.

In 1882, on Brücke's advice, Freud reluctantly left the laboratory to take a lowly post at the Vienna General Hospital. The reason was romantic: in April, he had met Martha Bernays, a slender, attractive young woman from northern Germany visiting one of his sisters, and fallen passionately in love. He was soon secretly engaged to her, but too poor to establish the respectable bourgeois household that he and his fiancée thought essential. It was not until September 1886, some five months after opening his practice in Vienna, with the aid of wedding gifts and loans from affluent friends, that the couple could marry. Within nine years, they had six children, the last of whom, Anna, grew up to be her father's confidante, secretary, nurse, disciple, and representative, and an eminent psychoanalyst in her own right.

Before his marriage, from October 1885 to February 1886, Freud worked in Paris with the celebrated French neurologist Jean-Martin Charcot, who impressed Freud with his bold advocacy of hypnosis as an instrument for healing medical disorders, and no less bold championship of the thesis (then quite unfashionable) that hysteria is an ailment to which men are susceptible no less than women. Charcot, an unrivaled observer, stimulated Freud's growing interest in the theoretical and therapeutic aspects of mental healing. Nervous ailments became Freud's specialty, and in the 1890s, as he told a friend, psychology became his tyrant. During these years he founded the psychoanalytic theory of mind.

He had intriguing if somewhat peculiar help. In 1887, he had met a nose-and-throat specialist from Berlin, Wilhelm Fliess, and rapidly established an intimate friendship with him. Fliess was the listener the lonely Freud craved: an intellectual gambler shocked at no idea, a propagator of provocative (at times fruitful) theories, an enthusiast who fed Freud ideas on which he could build. For over a decade, Fliess and Freud exchanged confidential letters and techni- cal memoranda, meeting occasionally to explore their sub- versive notions. And Freud was propelled toward the discov- ery of psychoanalysis in his practice: his patients proved excellent teachers. He was increasingly specializing in women suffering from hysteria, and, observing their symp- toms and listening to their complaints, he found that, though a good listener, he did not listen carefully enough. They had much to tell him.

In 1895, Freud and his fatherly friend Josef Breuer, a thriving, generous internist, published *Studies on Hysteria,* assigning Breuer's former patient "Anna O." pride of place. She had furnished fascinating material for intimate conver- sations between Breuer and Freud, and was to become, quite against her—and Breuer's—will, the founding patient of psychoanalysis. She demonstrated to Freud's satisfaction that hysteria originates in sexual malfunctioning and that symptoms can be talked away.

The year 1895 was decisive for Freud in other ways. In July, Freud managed to analyze a dream, his own, fully. He would employ this dream, known as "Irma's injection," as a model for psychoanalytic dream interpretation when he published it, some four years later, in his *Interpretation of*

Dreams. In the fall, he drafted, but neither completed nor published, what was later called the Project for a Scientific Psychology. It anticipated some of his fundamental theories yet serves as a reminder that Freud had been deeply enmeshed in the traditional physiological interpretation of mental events.

Increasingly Freud was offering psychological explanations for psychological phenomena. In the spring of 1896, he first used the fateful name, "psychoanalysis." Then in October his father died; "the most important event," he recalled a dozen years later, "the most poignant loss, of a man's life."[3] It supplied a powerful impetus toward psychoanalytic theorizing, stirring Freud to his unprecedented self-analysis, more systematic and thoroughgoing than the frankest autobiographer's self-probing. In the next three or four years, as he labored over his "Dream book," new discoveries crowded his days. But first he had to jettison the "seduction theory" he had championed for some time. It held that *every* neurosis results from premature sexual activity, mainly child molestation, in childhood.[4] Once freed from this far-reaching but improbable theory, Freud could appreciate the share of fantasies in mental life, and discover the Oedipus complex, that universal family triangle.

Freud's *Interpretation of Dreams* was published in November 1899.[5] It treated all dreams as wish fulfillments, detailed the mental stratagems that translate their causes into the strange drama the awakening dreamer remembers,

---

[3] Ibid., xxvi.

[4] Freud never claimed that sexual abuse does not exist. He had patients who he knew had not imagined the assaults they reported. All he abandoned when he abandoned the seduction theory was the sweeping claim that *only* the rape of a child, whether a boy or a girl, by a servant, an older sibling, or a classmate, could be the cause of a neurosis.

[5] The book bears the date of 1900 on the title page and this date is usually given as the date of publication.

and, in the difficult seventh chapter, outlined a comprehensive theory of mind. Its first reception was cool. During six years, only 351 copies were sold; a second edition did not appear until 1909. However, Freud's popularly written *Psychopathology of Everyday Life* of 1901 found a wider audience. Its collection of appealing slips of all sorts made Freud's fundamental point that the mind, however disheveled it might appear, is governed by firm rules. Thus—to give but one typical instance—the presiding officer of the Austrian parliament, facing a disagreeable season, opened it with the formal declaration that it was hereby closed. That "accident" had been prompted by his hidden repugnance for the sessions ahead.

Gradually, though still considered a radical, Freud acquired prestige and supporters. He had quarreled with Fliess in 1900, and, though their correspondence lingered on for some time, the two men never met again. Yet in 1902, after unconscionable delays, apparently generated by anti-Semitism combined with distrust of the maverick innovator, he was finally appointed an associate professor at the University of Vienna. Late that year, Freud and four other Viennese physicians began meeting every Wednesday night in his apartment at Berggasse 19 to discuss psychoanalytic questions; four years after, the group, grown to over a dozen regular participants, employed a paid secretary (Otto Rank) to take minutes and keep records. Finally, in 1908, it was transformed into the Vienna Psychoanalytic Society. At least some medical men (and a few women) were taking Freud's ideas seriously.

In 1905, Freud buttressed the structure of psychoanalytic thought with the second pillar of his theory: the *Three Essays on the Theory of Sexuality*. It outlined perversions and "normal" development from childhood to puberty with a lack of censoriousness and an openness hitherto virtually unknown. in medical literature. Again in 1905, Freud brought out his book on jokes and the first of his famous case histories: "Fragment of an Analysis of a Case of Hysteria," nicknamed the "Dora case." He published it to illustrate the uses of dream interpretation in psychoanalysis, and expose his failure to recognize the power of transference in the analytic situation, but its lack of empathy with his embattled teen-age analysand has made it controversial.

In the following decade, Freud enriched the technique of psychoanalysis with three more sophisticated case histories—"Analysis of a Phobia in a Five-Year-Old Boy" ("Little Hans"), "Notes upon a Case of Obsessional Neurosis" ("Rat Man") in 1909, and "Psycho-Analytic Notes on an Autobiographical Account of a Case of Paranoia" ("Schreber Case") in 1911. Despite recent reanalyses, they remain lucid expository models across a wide spectrum of mental ailments. Then, from 1910 on, Freud published pioneering, exceedingly influential papers on technique, to establish psychoanalytic method on sound foundations. Nor did he neglect theory; witness such an important paper as "Formulations on the Two Principles of Mental Functioning" (1911), in which he differentiated between the "primary process," the primitive, unconscious element in the mind, and the "secondary process," largely conscious and controlled.

During these years, Freud also broke out of the circumscribed bounds of clinical and theoretical specialization by publishing papers on religion, literature, sexual mores, biography, sculpture, prehistory, and much else. "Obsessive Actions and Religious Practices" (1907), "Creative Writers and Daydreaming" (1908), " 'Civilized' Sexual Morality and Modern Nervous Illness" (1908), and his widely debated study of the origins of homosexuality, "Leonardo da Vinci and a Memory of His Childhood" (1910), are only samples of his range. Freud took all of culture as his province. He was realizing the program he had outlined for himself in his youth: to solve some of the great riddles of human existence.

Yet Freud also found the decade from 1905 to 1914 agitating with the progress of, and disagreeable splits within, a rapidly emerging international movement—*his* movement. Psychoanalytic politics took center stage. Two principal sources of hope for the future of Freud's ideas, and later of envenomed contention, were the intelligent, Socialist Viennese physician Alfred Adler (1870–1937), and the original, self-willed Swiss psychiatrist Carl G. Jung (1875–1961). Adler had been among Freud's earliest adherents and remained for some years his most prominent Viennese advocate. But as professional interest in psychoanalysis—not all of it benevolent—grew apace, as Freud's upsetting ideas were being explored at psychiatrists' congresses, Freud aspired to enlarge the reach of psychoanalysis beyond its place of origin. Vienna, with its handful of followers, struck him as provincial, unsuitable as headquarters.

The first breakthrough came in 1906, when Jung, then principal psychiatrist at the renowned clinic Burghölzli in Zurich, sent Freud an offprint. Freud responded promptly; a cordial correspondence blossomed, and the friendship was cemented by Jung's visit to Freud in early 1907. Freud was only fifty, vigorous and productive, but he had long brooded on himself as aging and decrepit. He was seeking a successor who would carry the psychoanalytic dispensation to later generations and into a world larger than the Viennese, Jewish ambiance to which psychoanalysis was then confined. Jung, a formidable presence and energetic debater, was an inspired discovery: he was not old, he was not Viennese, he was not Jewish. Jung was prominent in the first international congress of psychoanalysts at Salzburg in the spring of 1908, and was appointed, the following year, editor of a newly

founded *Yearbook*. Freud, delighted with Jung, anointed
him his son, his crown prince—accolades that Jung wel
comed, indeed encouraged. Hence, when the International
Psychoanalytic Association was founded in March 1910, in
Nürnberg, Jung was Freud's logical, inevitable, choice for
president. Freud's Viennese adherents saw their city displaced by Zurich as the center of psychoanalysis, and did not
like it. A compromise was hammered out, and for some time
peace reigned in the Vienna Psychoanalytic Society. But
Adler was developing distinctive psychological ideas, which
featured aggressiveness over sexuality, and "organ inferiority" as a dominant cause of neuroses. A split became inevitable, and, in the summer of 1911, Adler and some of his
adherents resigned, leaving Freud and the Freudians in control of the Vienna society.

Freud was not without accolades. In September 1909, he
had received an honorary doctorate at Clark University in
Worcester, Massachusetts, as had Jung. But like Adler, Jung
increasingly diverged from Freud's ideas. He had never been
easy with the prominence Freud assigned to the sexual
drive—libido. By early 1912, these reservations took a personal turn. In response, Ernest Jones, Freud's principal English lieutenant, formed a defensive secret band of like-
minded analysts, the Committee. It consisted of himself,
Freud, Sandor Ferenczi (a brilliant adherent from Budapest), the witty Viennese lawyer Hanns Sachs, the astute
Berlin clinician and theorist Karl Abraham, and Freud's
amanuensis, the autodidact Otto Rank. It seemed needed:
by late 1912, the correspondence between Jung and Freud
had grown acrimonious and in January 1914, Freud ter-
minated his friendship with Jung. A split was only a matter
of time; in the spring of 1914, Jung resigned from his powerful positions in the psychoanalytic movement.

The strains of psychoanalytic politics did not keep Freud

from continuing his explorations of an impressive variety of topics. In 1913, he published an audacious, highly speculative venture into psychoanalytic prehistory, *Totem and Taboo*, which specified the moment that savages, in some dim, remote past, entered culture by murdering their father and acquiring guilt feelings. Then, in 1914, he published (anonymously) "The Moses of Michelangelo," uniting his admiration for Michelangelo's brooding sculpture with his powers of observation. In the same year, with an unsettling paper on narcissism, he subverted crucial aspects of psychoanalytic thought by throwing doubts upon his theory of drives—hitherto divided into erotic and egoistic.

But harrowing events on the world stage shouldered aside Freud's reassessment of psychoanalytic theory. On June 28, 1914, Austria's Archduke Francis Ferdinand and his consort were assassinated. Six weeks later, on August 4, Europe was at war. The first casualty for psychoanalysis was Freud's eventually best-known case history, "From the History of an Infantile Neurosis" ("Wolf Man"), written in the fall of 1914, but not published until 1918. Psychoanalytic activity almost ground to a halt. Many potential patients were at the front; most psychoanalysts were drafted into the medical corps; communications between "enemies" like Ernest Jones and Freud were severely truncated; psychoanalytic publications almost vanished; and congresses, the lifeblood of communication, were out of the question. For Freud, these were anxious times in other ways: all three of his sons were in the army, two of them almost daily in mortal danger.

Yet the war did not idle Freud's mind. Having too much time on his hands, he used it to good purpose. Work was a defense against brooding. Between March and July 1915, he wrote a dozen fundamental papers on metapsychology—on the unconscious, on repression, on melancholia; but he refused to gather them into the basic textbook he had planned. He published five of the papers between 1915 and 1917, and destroyed the rest. His enigmatic dissatisfaction with them hints at the discontent that had fueled his paper on narcissism. His map of the mind was inadequate to the evidence he had accumulated in his clinical experience. But he still lacked a satisfactory alternative. That would have to wait until after the war.

Another wartime activity, though more successful, gave Freud only modest pleasure: beginning in 1915, he delivered lectures at the university, published as a single volume in 1917 as *Introductory Lectures on Psycho-Analysis.* With the cunning of the born popularizer, Freud opened with a series on ordinary experiences, slips of the tongue, "unmotivated" forgetting, then turned to dreams and concluded with the technical topic, neuroses. Frequently reprinted and widely translated, these *Introductory Lectures* finally secured Freud a wide audience.

The war dragged on. Originally, somewhat to his surprise, an Austrian patriot, Freud wearied of the endless slaughter. He grew appalled at the chauvinism of intellectuals, the callousness of commanders, the stupidity of politicians. He had not yet fully acknowledged the theoretical significance of aggression, even though psychoanalysts had regularly encountered aggressiveness among their patients. But the war, beastly as it was, confirmed the skeptical psychoanalytic appraisal of human nature.

Signs of revived activity came shortly before the end of hostilities. In September 1918, for the first time since 1913, psychoanalysts from Germany and Austria-Hungary met in Budapest. Two months later, the war was over. To the family's immense relief, all of Freud's sons survived it. But the time for worry was far from over. The defeated powers were faced with revolution, drastically transformed from empires into republics, and saddled with stringent, vindictive peace treaties stripping them of territory and resources. Vienna was hungry, cold, desperate; food and fuel shortages produced deadly ailments—tuberculosis and influenza. In this stressful situation, Freud, who wasted no tears on the departed Hapsburg Empire, proved an energetic, imaginative manager. The portrait of Martha Freud shielding Herr Professor from domestic realities needs revision. Freud dispatched precise requests abroad to relatives, friends, associates, specifying what nourishment and clothing his family needed most, and how to send packages safely. Then, in January 1920, postwar misery struck home with deadly force: Freud's beloved second daughter Sophie, married and living in Hamburg, mother of two children, died in the influenza epidemic.

It has been plausibly argued that her death suggested the pessimistic drive theory that Freud now developed. Actually, he had virtually completed *Beyond the Pleasure Principle* (1920), which first announced Freud's theory of the death drive, the year before. Once Freud had adopted this construct, in which the forces of life, Eros, dramatically confront the forces of death, Thanatos, he found himself unable to think any other way. In 1923, in his classic study *The Ego and the Id*, he completed his revisions. He now proposed a "structural theory" of the mind, which visualizes the mind as divided into three distinct yet interacting agencies: the id (the wholly unconscious domain of the mind, consisting of the drives and of material later repressed), the ego (which is partly conscious and contains the defense mechanisms and the capacities to calculate, reason, and plan), and the super-ego (also only partly conscious, which harbors the conscience and, beyond that, unconscious feelings of guilt). This new scheme did not lead Freud to abandon his classic characterization of mental activity— emphasizing the distance of thoughts from awareness—as either conscious, or preconscious, or wholly unconscious. But he now made the decisive point that many of the mental operations of the ego, and of the super-ego as well, are inaccessible to direct introspection.

Meanwhile, the psychoanalytic movement was flourishing. Freud was becoming a household word, though he detested the sensationalized attention the popular press gave him. Better: in 1920, at the first postwar congress at The Hague, former "enemies" met as friends. Freud was accompanied by his daughter Anna, whom he was then analyzing and who joined the Vienna Psychoanalytic Society in 1922. In that year, the analysts convened in Berlin. It was the last congress Freud ever attended. In April 1923, he was operated on for a growth in his palate. While for months his doctors and closest associates pretended that the growth was benign, by September the truth was out: he had cancer. Severe operations followed in the fall. From then on Freud, compelled to wear a prosthesis, was rarely free of discomfort or pain.

But he never stopped working. While he had trouble speaking, he continued to analyze patients, many of them American physicians who came to Vienna as his "pupils" and returned to analyze in New York or Chicago. He continued to revise his theories. From the mid-1920s on, he wrote controversial papers on female sexuality, and, in 1926, *Inhibitions, Symptoms, and Anxiety,* which reversed his earlier thinking on anxiety, now treating it as a danger signal. Moreover, he wrote essays that found a relatively wide public: *The Future of an Illusion,* a convinced atheist's dissection of religion, in 1927, and, in 1930, *Civilization and Its Discontents,* a disillusioned look at modern civilization on the verge of catastrophe.

In 1933, that catastrophe came. On January 30, Hitler was appointed chancellor in Germany, and from then on

Austrian Nazis, already active, increasingly intervened in politics. The old guard was disappearing: Karl Abraham had died prematurely in 1925; Sandor Ferenczi followed him in 1933. Freud's closest friends were gone. But Freud was unwilling to leave the Vienna he hated and loved: he was too old, he did not want to desert, and besides, the Nazis would never invade his country. On the morning of March 12, 1938, the Germans proved him wrong. As the Nazis marched in, a jubilant populace greeted them. Spontaneous anti-Semitic outrages surpassed anything Germans had witnessed after five years of Nazi rule. Late in March, Anna was summoned to Gestapo headquarters; while she was released unharmed, the trauma changed Freud's mind: he must emigrate. It took months to satisfy the Nazi government's extortions, but on June 4, Freud left for Paris, welcomed by his former analysand and loving disciple, Princess Marie Bonaparte. On June 6, Freud landed in London, preceded by most of his family, "to die in freedom."

Aged and ill, he kept on working. Freud's last completed book, *Moses and Monotheism,* irritated and dismayed his Jewish readers with its assertion that Moses had been an Egyptian: he ended life as he had lived it—a disturber of the peace. He died bravely on September 23, 1939, asking his physician for a lethal dose of morphine. Freud did not believe in personal immortality, but his work lives on.

ABOUT THIS BOOK

In 1920, in *Beyond the Pleasure Principle,* Freud developed what came to be called the "structural theory" of mind, which portrays two fundamental drives, libido, or the drive toward life, and the death drive, wrestling with one another for preeminence, and which shows the three central institutions of the mind, the id, the ego, and the super-ego, as all at least partly unconscious. Three years later, in the present volume, he worked out important implications of these ideas. It must rank as the most significant work of Freud's later years. While highly theoretical, *The Ego and the Id* is, as Freud put it in the preface, "closer to psycho-analysis," closer to clinical experience, than its predecessor of 1920. It is worth noting that he might well have called this little book "The Ego, the Id, and the Super-Ego," for he gives the last of this trio some detailed discussion. Yet the heart of his concern is the ego, which he sees battling with three forces: the id, the super-ego, and the outside world. He never quite settled the question of its powers—much work on that and related matters was to be done after his death, by psychoanalytic theorists like Heinz Hartmann, Ernst Kris, and Rudolph Loewenstein—but in this text he sees it as a rider who pretty much goes where the horse wants to go.

EDITOR'S INTRODUCTION

Das Ich und das Es

(a) GERMAN EDITIONS:

1923   Leipzig, Vienna and Zurich: Internationaler Psychoanalytischer Verlag. Pp. 77.
1925   *G.S.*, 6, 351–405.
1931   *Theoretische Schriften*, 338–91.
1940   *G.W.*, 13, 237–289.

(b) ENGLISH TRANSLATION:
The Ego and the Id

1927   London: Hogarth Press and Institute of Psycho-Analysis. Pp. 88. (Tr. Joan Riviere.)
1961   *S.E.*, 19, 3–66. (Largely modified version of above.)

The present translation is a corrected reprint of the Standard Edition version.

This book appeared in the third week of April, 1923, though it had been in Freud's mind since at least the previous July (Jones, 1957, 104). On September 26, 1922, at the Seventh International Psycho-Analytical Congress, which was held in Berlin and was the last he ever attended, he read a short paper with the title 'Etwas vom Unbewussten [Some

Remarks on the Unconscious]', in which he foreshadowed the contents of the book. An abstract of this paper (which was never itself published) appeared that autumn in the *Int. Zeitschrift Psychoanal.*, 5 (4), 486,[1] and, although there is no certainty that it was written by Freud himself, it is worth while recording it:

'Some Remarks on the Unconscious'

'The speaker repeated the familiar history of the development of the concept "unconscious" in psycho-analysis. "Unconscious" was in the first instance a purely descriptive term which accordingly included what is temporarily latent. The dynamic view of the process of repression made it necessary, however, to give the unconscious a systematic sense, so that the unconscious had to be equated with the repressed. What is latent and only temporarily unconscious received the name of "preconscious" and, from the systematic point of view, was brought into close proximity to the conscious. The double meaning of the term "unconscious" undoubtedly involved disadvantages, though they were of little significance and were difficult to avoid. It has turned out, however, that it is not practicable to regard the repressed as coinciding with the unconscious and the ego with the preconscious and conscious. The speaker discussed the two facts which show that in the ego too there is an unconscious, which behaves dynamically like the repressed unconscious: the two facts of a resistance proceeding from the ego during analysis and of an unconscious sense of guilt. He announced that in a book which was shortly to appear—*The Ego and the Id*—he had

---

[1] A translation was published in the *Int. J. Psycho-Anal.* the next year, 4 (3), 367. (The date of the reading of the paper is there misprinted 'Sept. 25'.) It is reprinted here in a slightly modified form.

made an attempt to estimate the influence which these new discoveries must have upon our view of the unconscious.'

The Ego and the Id is the last of Freud's major theoretical works. It offers a description of the mind and its workings which is at first sight new and even revolutionary; and indeed all psycho-analytic writings that date from after its publication bear the unmistakable imprint of its effects—at least in regard to their terminology. But, in spite of all its fresh insights and fresh syntheses, we can trace, as so often with Freud's apparent innovations, the seeds of his new ideas in earlier, and sometimes in far earlier, writings.

The forerunners of the present general picture of the mind had been successively the 'Project' of 1895 (Freud, 1950a), the seventh chapter of *The Interpretation of Dreams* (1900a) and the metapsychological papers of 1915. In all of these, the interrelated problems of mental functioning and mental structure were inevitably considered, though with varying stress upon the two aspects of the question. The historical accident that psycho-analysis had its origin in connection with the study of hysteria led at once to the hypothesis of repression (or, more generally, of defence) as a mental function, and this in turn to a topographical hypothesis—to a picture of the mind as including two portions, one repressed and the other repressing. The quality of 'consciousness' was evidently closely involved in these hypotheses; and it was easy to equate the repressed part of the mind with what was 'unconscious' and the repressing part with what was 'conscious'. Freud's earlier pictorial diagrams of the mind, in *The Interpretation of Dreams* (*Standard Ed.*, 5, 537–41) and in his letter to Fliess of December 6, 1896 (Freud, 1950a, Letter 52), were representations of this view of the position. And this apparently simple scheme underlay all of Freud's earlier theoretical ideas: functionally, a repressed force endeavouring to make its way into activity but held in check by a repressing force, and structurally, an 'unconscious' opposed by an 'ego'.

Nevertheless, complications soon became manifest. It was quickly seen that the word 'unconscious' was being used in two senses: the 'descriptive' sense (which merely attributed a particular *quality* to a mental state) and the 'dynamic' sense (which attributed a particular *function* to a mental state). This distinction was already stated, though not in these terms, in *The Interpretation of Dreams* (*Standard Ed.*, 5, 614–15). It was stated much more clearly in the English paper written for the Society for Psychical Research (1912g, ibid., 12, 262). But from the first another, more obscure notion was already involved (as was plainly shown by the pictorial diagrams)—the notion of 'systems' in the mind. This implied a topographical or structural division of the mind based on something more than function, a division into portions to which it was possible to attribute a number of differentiating characteristics and methods of operating. Some such idea was no doubt already implied in the phrase 'the unconscious', which appeared very early (e.g. in a footnote to the *Studies on Hysteria*, 1895d, *Standard Ed.*, 2, 76). The concept of a 'system' became explicit in *The Interpretation of Dreams* (1900a), ibid., 5, 536–7. From the terms in which it was there introduced, topographical imagery was at once suggested, though Freud gave a warning against taking this literally. There were a number of these 'systems' (mnemic, perceptual, and so on) and among them 'the unconscious' (ibid., 541), which 'for simplicity's sake' was to be designated as 'the system *Ucs.*'. In these earlier passages all that was overtly meant by this unconscious system was the repressed, until we reach the final section of *The Interpretation of Dreams* (ibid., 5, 611 ff.), where something with a much wider scope was indicated. Thereafter the question remained in abeyance until the S.P.R. paper (1912*g*) already referred to, where (besides the clear differentiation between the descriptive and dynamic uses of the term 'unconscious'), in the last sentences of the paper, a third, 'systematic', use was defined. It may be noted that in this passage (ibid., **12**, 266), it was only for this 'systematic' unconscious that Freud proposed to use the symbol '*Ucs.*'. All this seems very straightforward, but, oddly enough, the picture was blurred once more in the metapsychological paper on 'The Unconscious' (1915*e*). In Section II of that paper (ibid., **14**, 172 ff.) there were no longer *three* uses of the term 'unconscious' but only two. The 'dynamic' use disappeared, and was presumably subsumed into the 'systematic' one,[2] which was still to be called the '*Ucs.*', though it now included the repressed. Finally, in Chapter I of the present work (as well as in Lecture XXXI of the *New Introductory Lectures*, 1933*a*) Freud reverted to the threefold distinction and classification, though at the end of the chapter he applied the abbreviation '*Ucs.*', inadvertently perhaps, to all three kinds of 'unconscious' (p. 8).

But the question now arose whether, as applied to a *system*, the term 'unconscious' was at all appropriate. In the structural picture of the mind what had from the first been most clearly differentiated from 'the unconscious' had been 'the ego'. And it now began to appear that the ego itself ought partly to be described as 'unconscious'. This was pointed out in *Beyond the Pleasure Principle*, in a sentence which read in the first edition (1920*g*): 'It may be that much of the ego is itself unconscious[3]; only a part of it, probably, is covered by the term "preconscious".' In the second edi-

---

[2]The two terms seem to be definitely equated in *Beyond the Pleasure Principle* (1920*g*), ibid., **18**, 20; *I.P.L.*, **4**, 14.
[3][I.e. not merely in the descriptive but also in the dynamic sense.]

tion, a year later, this sentence was altered to: 'It is certain that much of the ego is itself unconscious . . .; only a small part of it is covered by the term "preconscious".'[4] And this discovery and the grounds for it were stated with still greater insistence in the first chapter of the present work.

It had thus become apparent that, alike as regards 'the unconscious' and as regards 'the ego', the criterion of consciousness was no longer helpful in building up a structural picture of the mind. Freud accordingly abandoned the use of consciousness in this capacity: 'being conscious' was henceforward to be regarded simply as a quality which might or might not be attached to a mental state. The old 'descriptive' sense of the term was in fact all that remained. The new terminology which he now introduced had a highly clarifying effect and so made further clinical advances possible. But it did not in itself involve any fundamental changes in Freud's views on mental structure and functioning. Indeed, the three newly presented entities, the id, the ego and the super-ego, all had lengthy past histories (two of them under other names) and these will be worth examining.

The term *aas Es'*,[5] as Freud himself explains below (p. 17), was derived in the first instance from Georg Groddeck, a physician practising at Baden-Baden, who had recently become attached to psycho-analysis and with whose wide-ranging ideas Freud felt much sympathy. Groddeck seems in turn to have derived *'das Es'* from his own teacher, Ernst Schweninger, a well-known German physician of an earlier

---

[4] Freud had actually already spoken in the opening sentence of his second paper on "The Neuro-Psychoses of Defence' (1896*b*) of the psychical mechanism of defence as being 'unconscious'.

[5] There was to begin with a good deal of discussion over the choice of an English equivalent. 'The id' was eventually decided upon in preference to 'the it', so as to be parallel with the long-established 'ego'.

generation. But, as Freud also points out, the use of the word
certainly goes back to Nietzsche. In any case, the term was
adapted by Freud to a different and more precise meaning
than Groddeck's. It cleared up and in part replaced the
ill-defined uses of the earlier terms 'the unconscious', 'the
Ucs.' and 'the systematic unconscious'.[6]

The position in regard to *'das Ich'* is a good deal less clear.
The term had of course been in familiar use before the days
of Freud; but the precise sense which he himself attached
to it in his earlier writings is not unambiguous. It seems
possible to detect two main uses: one in which the term
distinguishes a person's self as a whole (including, perhaps,
his body) from other people, and the other in which it
denotes a particular part of the mind characterized by special attributes and functions. It is in this second sense that
the term was used in the elaborate account of the 'ego' in
Freud's early 'Project' of 1895 (Freud, 1950a, Part I, Section 14); and it is in this same sense that it is used in the
anatomy of the mind in *The Ego and the Id.* But in some
of his intervening works, particularly in connection with
narcissism, the 'ego' seems to correspond rather to the 'self'.
It is not always easy, however, to draw a line between these
two senses of the word.[7]

What is quite certain, however, is that, after the isolated

---

[6]The symbol *'Ucs.'* disappears after the present work, except for a single belated occurrence in *Moses and Monotheism* (1939a), Chapter III,
Part 1 (E), where oddly enough it is used in the 'descriptive' sense. Freud
continued to use the term 'the unconscious', though with diminishing
frequency, as a synonym for 'the id'.

[7]In a few places in the *Standard Edition* where the sense seemed to
demand it, *'das Ich'* has been translated by 'the self'. There is a passage
in *Civilization and its Discontents* (1930a), towards the beginning of the
fourth paragraph of Chapter I, in which Freud himself explicitly equates
'das Selbst' and *'das Ich.'* And, in the course of a discussion of the moral
responsibility for dreams (1925i), *S.E.,* 19, 133, he makes a clear distinction between the two uses of the German word *'Ich'.*

attempt in the 'Project' of 1895 at a detailed analysis of the structure and functioning of the ego, Freud left the subject almost untouched for some fifteen years. His interest was concentrated on his investigations of the unconscious and its instincts, particularly the sexual ones, and in the part they played in normal and abnormal mental behavior. The fact that repressive forces played an equally important part was, of course, never overlooked and was always insisted on; but the closer examination of them was left to the future. It was enough for the moment to give them the inclusive name of 'the ego'.

There were two indications of a change, both round about the year 1910. In a paper on psychogenic disturbances of vision (1910*i*), there comes what seems to be a first mention of 'ego-instincts' (*Standard Ed.*, 11, 214), which combine the functions of repression with those of self-preservation. The other and more important development was the hypothesis of narcissism which was first proposed in 1909 and which led the way to a detailed examination of the ego and its functions in a variety of connections—in the study on Leonardo (1910*c*), in the Schreber case history (1911*c*), in the paper on the two principles of mental functioning (1911*b*), in the paper on 'Narcissism' itself (1914*c*) and in the metapsychological paper on 'The Unconscious' (1915*e*). In this last work, however, a further development occurred: what had been described as the ego now became the 'system' *Cs.* (*Pcs.*).[8] It is this system which is the progenitor of the 'ego' as we have it in the new and corrected terminology, from which, as we have seen, the confusing connection with the quality of 'consciousness' has been removed.

The functions of the system *Cs.* (*Pcs.*), as enumerated in

---

[8] These abbreviations (like the '*Ucs.*') go back to *The Interpretation of Dreams* (1900*a*), *Standard Ed.*, 5, 540 *n.*

'The Unconscious', *Standard Ed.*, 14, 188, include such activities as censorship, reality-testing and so on, all of which are now assigned to the 'ego'. There is one particular function, however, whose examination was to lead to momentous results—the self-critical faculty. This and the correlated 'sense of guilt' attracted Freud's interest from early days, chiefly in connection with the obsessional neurosis. His theory that obsessions are 'transformed self-reproaches' for sexual pleasure enjoyed in childhood was fully explained in Section II of his second paper on 'The Neuro-Psychoses of Defence' (1896*b*) after being outlined somewhat earlier in his letters to Fliess. That the self-reproaches may be unconscious was already implied at this stage, and was stated specifically in the paper on 'Obsessive Actions and Religious Practices' (1907*b*), *Standard Ed.*, 9, 123. It was only with the concept of narcissism, however, that light could be thrown on the actual mechanism of these self reproaches. In Section III of his paper on narcissism (1914*c*) Freud began by suggesting that the narcissism of infancy is replaced in the adult by devotion to an ideal ego set up within himself. He then put forward the notion that there may be 'a special psychical agency' whose task it is to watch the actual ego and measure it by the ideal ego or ego ideal—he seemed to use the terms indiscriminately (*Standard Ed.*, 14, 95). He attributed a number of functions to this agency, including the normal conscience, the dream-censorship and certain paranoic delusions. In the paper on 'Mourning and Melancholia' (1917*e* [1915]) he further made this agency responsible for pathological states of mourning (ibid., 14, 247) and insisted more definitely that it is something apart from the rest of the ego, and this was made still more clear in *Group Psychology* (1921*c*). It must be noticed, however, that here the distinction between the 'ego ideal' itself and the 'agency' concerned with its enforcement had been dropped: the 'agency' was specifically called the 'ego ideal' (*Standard Ed.*, 18, 109–10). It is as an equivalent to the 'ego ideal' that *'das Uber-Ich'*[9] makes its first appearance (p. 22 below), though its aspect as an enforcing or prohibiting agency predominates later. Indeed, after *The Ego and the Id* and the two or three shorter works immediately following it, the 'ego ideal' disappears almost completely as a technical term. It makes a brief re-emergence in a couple of sentences in the *New Introductory Lectures* (1933*a*), Lecture XXXI; but here we find a return to the original distinction, for 'an important function' attributed to the super-ego is to act as 'the vehicle of the ego ideal by which the ego measures itself'—almost the exact terms in which the ego ideal was first introduced in the paper on narcissism (*Standard Ed.*, 14, 93).

But this distinction may seem to be an artificial one when we turn to Freud's account of the genesis of the super-ego. This account (in Chapter III) is no doubt the part of the book second in importance only to the main thesis of the threefold division of the mind. The super-ego is there shown to be derived from a transformation of the child's earliest object-cathexes into identifications: it takes the place of the Oedipus complex. This mechanism (the replacement of an object-cathexis by an identification and the introjection of the former object) had been first applied by Freud (in his study of Leonardo, 1910*c*) to the explanation of one type of homosexuality, in which a boy replaces his love for his mother by identifying himself with her (*Standard Ed.*, 11, 100). He next applied the same notion to states of depression in 'Mourning and Melancholia' (1917*e*), ibid., 14, 249.

---

[9]Jones (1957, 305 *n.*) remarks that the term had been used earlier by Münsterberg (1908), though, he adds, it was in a different sense and it is unlikely that Freud had come across the passage.

Further and more elaborate discussions of these various kinds of identifications and introjections were pursued in Chapters VII, VIII and XI of *Group Psychology* (1921c), but it was only in the present work that Freud arrived at his final views on the derivation of the super-ego from the child's earliest object-relations.

Having once established his new account of the anatomy of the mind, Freud was in a position to examine its implications, and this he already does in the later pages of the book—the relation between the divisions of the mind and the two classes of instincts, and the interrelations between the divisions of the mind themselves, with special reference to the sense of guilt. But many of these questions, and in particular the last one, were to form the subject of other writings which followed in rapid succession. See, for instance, 'The Economic Problem of Masochism' (1924c), 'The Dissolution of the Oedipus Complex' (1924d), the two papers on neurosis and psychosis (1924b and 1924e), and the one on the anatomical distinction between the sexes (1925j) (all in *Standard Ed.*, 19), as well as the still more important *Inhibitions, Symptoms and Anxiety* (1926d), published only a little later. Finally, a further long discussion of the super-ego, together with an interesting examination of the proper use of the terms 'super-ego', 'conscience', 'sense of guilt', 'need for punishment' and 'remorse' will be found in Chapters VII and VIII of *Civilization and its Discontents* (1930a).

Extracts from the earlier (1927) translation of this work were included in Rickman's *General Selection from the Works of Sigmund Freud* (1937, 245–74).

Editorial additions, whether to the text or the footnotes, are printed in square brackets.

Preface

The present discussions are a further development of some trains of thought which I opened up in *Beyond the Pleasure Principle* (1920g), and to which, as I remarked there,[1] my attitude was one of a kind of benevolent curiosity. In the following pages these thoughts are linked to various facts of analytic observation and an attempt is made to arrive at new conclusions from this conjunction; in the present work, however, there are no fresh borrowings from biology, and on that account it stands closer to psycho-analysis than does *Beyond the Pleasure Principle*. It is more in the nature of a synthesis than of a speculation and seems to have had an ambitious aim in view. I am conscious, however, that it does not go beyond the roughest outline and with that limitation I am perfectly content.

In these pages things are touched on which have not yet been the subject of psycho-analytic consideration, and it has not been possible to avoid trenching upon some theories which have been put forward by non-analysts or by former analysts on their retreat from analysis. I have elsewhere always been ready to acknowledge what I owe to other workers; but in this instance I feel burdened by no such debt

---

[1][*Standard Ed.*, **18**, 59; *I.P.L.*, **4**, 53.]

of gratitude. If psycho-analysis has not hitherto shown its appreciation of certain things, this has never been because it overlooked their achievement or sought to deny their importance, but because it followed a particular path, which had not yet led so far. And finally, when it has reached them, things have a different look to it from what they have to others.

THE EGO
AND THE ID

I

Consciousness and What Is Unconscious

In this introductory chapter there is nothing new to be said and it will not be possible to avoid repeating what has often been said before.

The division of the psychical into what is conscious and what is unconscious is the fundamental premiss of psycho-analysis; and it alone makes it possible for psycho-analysis to understand the pathological processes in mental life, which are as common as they are important, and to find a place for them in the framework of science. To put it once more, in a different way: psycho-analysis cannot situate the essence of the psychical in consciousness, but is obliged to regard consciousness as a quality of the psychical, which may be present in addition to other qualities or may be absent.

If I could suppose that everyone interested in psychology would read this book, I should also be prepared to find that at this point some of my readers would already stop short and would go no further; for here we have the first shibboleth of psycho-analysis. To most people who have been educated in philosophy the idea of anything psychical which is not also conscious is so inconceivable that it seems to them absurd and refutable simply by logic. I believe this is only because they have never studied the relevant phenomena of hypnosis and dreams, which—quite apart from pathological manifestations—necessitate this view. Their psychology of consciousness is incapable of solving the problems of dreams and hypnosis.

'Being conscious'[1] is in the first place a purely descriptive term, resting on perception of the most immediate and certain character. Experience goes on to show that a psychical element (for instance, an idea) is not as a rule conscious for a protracted length of time. On the contrary, a state of consciousness is characteristically very transitory; an idea that is conscious now is no longer so a moment later, although it can become so again under certain conditions that are easily brought about. In the interval the idea was—we do not know what. We can say that it was *latent*, and by this we mean that it was *capable of becoming conscious* at any time. Or, if we say that is was *unconscious*, we shall also be giving a correct description of it. Here 'unconscious' coincides with 'latent and capable of becoming conscious'. The philosophers would no doubt object: 'No, the term "unconscious" is not applicable here; so long as the idea was in a state of latency it was not anything psychical at all.' To contradict them at this point would lead to nothing more profitable than a verbal dispute.

But we have arrived at the term or concept of the unconscious along another path, by considering certain experiences in which mental *dynamics* play a part. We have found—that is, we have been obliged to assume—that very

---

[1]['*Bewusst sein*' (in two words) in the original. Similarly in Chapter II of *Lay Analysis* (1926e), *Standard Ed.*, 20, 197. '*Bewusstein*' is the regular German word for 'consciousness', and printing it in two words emphasizes the fact that '*bewusst*' is in its form a passive participle—'being conscioused'. The English 'conscious' is capable of an active or a passive use; but in these discussions it is always to be taken as passive. Cf. a footnote at the end of the Editor's Note to Freud's metapsychological paper on 'The Unconscious', *Standard Ed.*, 14, 165.]

powerful mental processes or ideas exist (and here a quantitative or *economic* factor comes into question for the first
time) which can produce all the effects in mental life that
ordinary ideas do (including effects that can in their turn
become conscious as ideas), though they themselves do not
become conscious. It is unnecessary to repeat in detail here
what has been explained so often before.[2] It is enough to say
that at this point psycho-analytic theory steps in and asserts
that the reason why such ideas cannot become conscious is
that a certain force opposes them, that otherwise they could
become conscious, and that it would then be apparent how
little they differ from other elements which are admittedly
psychical. The fact that in the technique of psycho-analysis
a means has been found by which the opposing force can be
removed and the ideas in question made conscious renders
this theory irrefutable. The state in which the ideas existed
before being made conscious is called by us *repression*, and
we assert that the force which instituted the repression and
maintains it is perceived as *resistance* during the work of
analysis.

Thus we obtain our concept of the unconscious from the
theory of repression. The repressed is the prototype of the
unconscious for us. We see, however, that we have two kinds
of unconscious—the one which is latent but capable of
becoming conscious, and the one which is repressed and
which is not, in itself and without more ado, capable of
becoming conscious. This piece of insight into psychical
dynamics cannot fail to affect terminology and description.
The latent, which is unconscious only descriptively, not in
the dynamic sense, we call *preconscious;* we restrict the term

---

[2][See, for instance, 'A Note on the Unconscious' (1912g), *Standard Ed.*,
12, 262 and 264.]

[margin annotations: why things become conscious; repression and resistance]

[handwritten note at bottom: we obtain our concept of the unconscious from the theory of repression.]

Pcs., Ucs., Cs.

unconscious to the dynamically unconscious repressed; so that now we have three terms, conscious (*Cs.*), preconscious (*Pcs.*), and unconscious (*Ucs.*), whose sense is no longer purely descriptive. The *Pcs.* is presumably a great deal closer to the *Cs.* than is the *Ucs.*, and since we have called the *Ucs.* psychical we shall with even less hesitation call the latent *Pcs.* psychical. But why do we not rather, instead of this, remain in agreement with the philosophers and, in a consistent way, distinguish the *Pcs.* as well as the *Ucs.* from the conscious psychical? The philosophers would then propose that the *Pcs.* and the *Ucs.* should be described as two species or stages of the 'psychoid', and harmony would be established. But endless difficulties in exposition would follow; and the one important fact, that these two kinds of 'psychoid' coincide in almost every other respect with what is admittedly psychical, would be forced into the background in the interests of a prejudice dating from a period in which these psychoids, or the most important part of them, were still unknown.

We can now play about comfortably with our three terms, *Cs., Pcs., and Ucs.*, so long as we do not forget that in the descriptive sense there are two kinds of unconscious, but in the dynamic sense only one.[3] For purposes of exposition this distinction can in some cases be ignored, but in others it is of course indispensable. At the same time, we have become more or less accustomed to this ambiguity of the unconscious and have managed pretty well with it. As far as I can see, it is impossible to avoid this ambiguity; the distinction between conscious and unconscious is in the last resort a question of perception, which must be answered 'yes' or 'no', and the act of perception itself tells us nothing of the

---

[3][Some comments on this sentence will be found in Appendix A (p. 63).]

reason why a thing is or is not perceived. No one has a right to complain because the actual phenomenon expresses the dynamic factor ambiguously.[4]

---

[4] This may be compared so far with my 'Note on the Unconscious in Psycho-Analysis' (1912g). [Cf. also Sections I and II of the metapsychological paper on 'The Unconscious' (1915e).] A new turn taken by criticisms of the unconscious deserves consideration at this point. Some investigators, who do not refuse to recognize the facts of psycho-analysis but who are unwilling to accept the unconscious, find a way out of the difficulty in the fact, which no one contests, that in consciousness (regarded as a phenomenon) it is possible to distinguish a great variety of gradations in intensity or clarity. Just as there are processes which are very vividly, glaringly, and tangibly conscious, so we also experience others which are only faintly, hardly even noticeably conscious; those that are most faintly conscious are, it is argued, the ones to which psycho-analysis wishes to apply the unsuitable name 'unconscious'. These too, however (the argument proceeds), are conscious or 'in consciousness', and can be made fully and intensely conscious if sufficient attention is paid to them.

In so far as it is possible to influence by arguments the decision of a question of this kind which depends either on convention or on emotional factors, we may make the following comments. The reference to gradations of clarity in consciousness is in no way conclusive and has no more evidential value than such analogous statements as: 'There are so very many gradations in illumination—from the most glaring and dazzling light to the dimmest glimmer—therefore there is no such thing as darkness at all'; or, 'There are varying degrees of vitality, therefore there is no such thing as death.' Such statements may in a certain way have a meaning, but for practical purposes they are worthless. This will be seen if one tries to draw particular conclusions from them, such as, 'there is therefore no need to strike a light', or, 'therefore all organisms are immortal'. Further, to include 'what is unnoticeable' under the concept of 'what is conscious' is simply to play havoc with the one and only piece of direct and certain knowledge that we have about the mind. And after all, a consciousness of which one knows nothing seems to me a good deal more absurd than something mental that is unconscious. Finally, this attempt to equate what is unnoticed with what is unconscious is obviously made without taking into account the dynamic conditions involved, which were the decisive factors in forming the psycho-analytic view. For it ignores two facts: first, that it is exceedingly difficult and requires very great effort to concentrate enough attention on something unnoticed of this kind; and secondly, that when this has been achieved the thought which was previously unnoticed is not

Ego: underlying principle

In the further course of psycho-analytic work, however, even these distinctions have proved to be inadequate and, for practical purposes, insufficient. This has become clear in more ways than one; but the decisive instance is as follows. We have formed the idea that in each individual there is a coherent organization of mental processes; and we call this his *ego*. It is to this ego that consciousness is attached; the ego controls the approaches to motility—that is, to the discharge of excitations into the external world; it is the mental agency which supervises all its own constituent processes, and which goes to sleep at night, though even then it exercises the censorship on dreams. From this ego proceed the repressions, too, by means of which it is sought to exclude certain trends in the mind not merely from consciousness but also from other forms of effectiveness and activity. In analysis these trends which have been shut out stand in opposition to the ego, and the analysis is faced with the task of removing the resistances which the ego displays against concerning itself with the repressed. Now we find during analysis that, when we put certain tasks before the patient, he gets into difficulties; his associations fail when they should be coming near the repressed. We then tell him that he is dominated by a resistance; but he is quite unaware of the fact, and, even if he guesses from his unpleasurable feelings that a resistance is now at work in him, he does not know what it is or how to describe it. Since, however, there can be no question but that this resistance emanates from his ego and belongs to it, we find ourselves in an unforeseen situation. We have come upon something in the ego itself

---

recognized by consciousness, but often seems entirely alien and opposed to it and is promptly disavowed by it. Thus, seeking refuge from the unconscious in what is scarcely noticed or unnoticed is after all only a derivative of the preconceived belief which regards the identity of the psychical and the conscious as settled once and for all.

which is also unconscious, which behaves exactly like the repressed—that is, which produces powerful effects without itself being conscious and which requires special work before it can be made conscious. From the point of view of analytic practice, the consequence of this discovery is that we land in endless obscurities and difficulties if we keep to our habitual forms of expression and try, for instance, to derive neuroses from a conflict between the conscious and the unconscious. We shall have to substitute for this antithesis another, taken from our insight into the structural conditions of the mind—the antithesis between the coherent ego and the repressed which is split off from it.[5]

For our conception of the unconscious, however, the consequences of our discovery are even more important. Dynamic considerations caused us to make our first correction; our insight into the structure of the mind leads to the second. We recognize that the *Ucs.* does not coincide with the repressed; it is still true that all that is repressed is *Ucs.*, but not all that is *Ucs.* is repressed. A part of the ego, too—and Heaven knows how important a part—may be *Ucs.*, undoubtedly is *Ucs.*[6] And this *Ucs.* belonging to the ego is not latent like the *Pcs.*; for if it were, it could not be activated without becoming *Cs.*, and the process of making it conscious would not encounter such great difficulties. When we find ourselves thus confronted by the necessity of postulating a third *Ucs.*, which is not repressed, we must admit that the characteristic of being unconscious begins to lose significance for us. It becomes a quality which can have many meanings, a quality which we are unable to make, as

---

[5]Cf. *Beyond the Pleasure Principle* (1920g) [*S.E.*, 18, 19; *I.P.L.*, 4, 13].
[6][This had already been stated not only in *Beyond the Pleasure Principle* (loc. cit.) but earlier, in 'The Unconscious' (1915e), *Standard Ed.*, 14, 192–3. Indeed, it was implied in a remark at the beginning of the second paper on 'The Neuro-Psychoses of Defence' (1896b).]

we should have hoped to do, the basis of far-reaching and inevitable conclusions. Nevertheless we must beware of ignoring this characteristic, for the property of being conscious or not is in the last resort our one beacon-light in the darkness of depth-psychology.

II

The Ego and the Id

———————

Pathological research has directed our interest too exclusively to the repressed. We should like to learn more about the ego, now that we know that it, too, can be unconscious in the proper sense of the word. Hitherto the only guide we have had during our investigations has been the distinguishing mark of being conscious or unconscious; we have finally come to see how ambiguous this can be.

Now all our knowledge is invariably bound up with consciousness. We can come to know even the *Ucs.* only by making it conscious. But stop, how is that possible? What does it mean when we say 'making something conscious'? How can that come about?

We already know the point from which we have to start in this connection. We have said that consciousness is the *surface* of the mental apparatus; that is, we have ascribed it as a function to a system which is spatially the first one reached from the external world—and spatially not only in the functional sense but, on this occasion, also in the sense of anatomical dissection.[1] Our investigations too must take this perceiving surface as a starting-point.

All perceptions which are received from without (sense-

———————

[1] *Beyond the Pleasure Principle* [*Standard Ed.*, 18, 26; *I.P.L.*, 4, 20].

perceptions) and from within—what we call sensations and feelings—are *Cs.* from the start. But what about those internal processes which we may—roughly and inexactly—sum up under the name of thought-processes? They represent displacements of mental energy which are effected somewhere in the interior of the apparatus as this energy proceeds on its way towards action. Do they advance to the surface, which causes consciousness to be generated? Or does consciousness make its way to them? This is clearly one of the difficulties that arise when one begins to take the spatial or 'topographical' idea of mental life seriously. Both these possibilities are equally unimaginable; there must be a third alternative.[2]

I have already, in another place,[3] suggested that the real difference between a *Ucs.* and a *Pcs.* idea (thought) consists in this: that the former is carried out on some material which remains unknown, whereas the latter (the *Pcs.*) is in addition brought into connection with word-presentations. This is the first attempt to indicate distinguishing marks for the two systems, the *Pcs.* and the *Ucs.*, other than their relation to consciousness. The question, 'How does a thing become conscious?' would thus be more advantageously stated: 'How does a thing become preconscious?' And the answer would be: 'Through becoming connected with the word-presentations corresponding to it.'

These word-presentations are residues of memories; they were at one time perceptions, and like all mnemic residues they can become conscious again. Before we concern ourselves further with their nature, it dawns upon us like a new discovery that only something which has once been a *Cs.*

---

[2][This had been discussed at greater length in the second section of 'The Unconscious' (1915*e*), *Standard Ed.*, 18, 173–6.]

[3]'The Unconscious' [ibid., 201 ff.].

How does a thing become Conscious?

word presentations

perception can become conscious, and that anything arising from within (apart from feelings) that seeks to become conscious must try to transform itself into external perceptions: this becomes possible by means of memory-traces.

We think of the mnemic residues as being contained in systems which are directly adjacent to the system *Pcpt.-Cs.*, so that the cathexes of those residues can readily extend from within on to the elements of the latter system.[4] We immediately think here of hallucinations, and of the fact that the most vivid memory is always distinguishable both from a hallucination and from an external perception;[5] but it will also occur to us at once that when a memory is revived the cathexis remains in the mnemic system, whereas a hallucination, which is not distinguishable from a perception, can arise when the cathexis does not merely spread over from the memory-trace on to the *Pcpt.* element, but passes over to it *entirely.*

Verbal residues are derived primarily from auditory perceptions,[6] so that the system *Pcs.* has, as it were, a special sensory source. The visual components of word-presentations are secondary, acquired through reading, and may to begin with be left on one side; so may the motor images of words, which, except with deaf-mutes, play the part of auxiliary indications. In essence a word is after all the mnemic residue of a word that has been heard.

We must not be led, in the interests of simplification perhaps, to forget the importance of optical mnemic resi-

---

[4][Cf. Chapter VII (B) of *The Interpretation of Dreams* (1900*a*), *Standard Ed.*, **5**, 538.]

[5][This view had been expressed by Breuer in his theoretical contribution to *Studies on Hysteria* (1895*d*), *Standard Ed.*, **2**, 188.]

[6][Freud had arrived at this conclusion in his monograph on aphasia (1891*b*) on the basis of pathological findings (ibid., 92–4). The point is represented in the diagram reproduced from that work in Appendix C to the paper on 'The Unconscious', *Standard Ed.*, **14**, 214.]

dues, when they are of *things,* or to deny that it is possible for thought-processes to become conscious through a reversion to visual residues, and that in many people this seems to be the favoured method. The study of dreams and of preconscious phantasies as shown in Varendonck's observations[7] can give us an idea of the special character of this visual thinking. We learn that what becomes conscious in it is as a rule only the concrete subject-matter of the thought, and that the relations between the various elements of this subject-matter, which is what specially characterizes thoughts, cannot be given visual expression. Thinking in pictures is, therefore, only a very incomplete form of becoming conscious. In some way, too, it stands nearer to unconscious processes than does thinking in words, and it is unquestionably older than the latter both ontogenetically and phylogenetically.

To return to our argument: if, therefore, this is the way in which something that is in itself unconscious becomes preconscious, the question how we make something that is repressed (pre)conscious would be answered as follows. It is done by supplying *Pcs.* intermediate links through the work of analysis. Consciousness remains where it is, therefore; but, on the other hand, the *Ucs.* does not rise into the *Cs.*

Whereas the relation of *external* perceptions to the ego is quite perspicuous, that of *internal* perceptions to the ego requires special investigation. It gives rise once more to a doubt whether we are really right in referring the whole of consciousness to the single superficial system *Pcpt.-Cs.*

Internal perceptions yield sensations of processes arising in the most diverse and certainly also in the deepest strata of the mental apparatus. Very little is known about these

---

[7][Cf. Varendonck (1921), a book to which Freud contributed an introduction (1921*b*).]

sensations and feelings; those belonging to the pleasure-unpleasure series may still be regarded as the best examples of them They are more primordial, more elementary, than perceptions arising externally and they can come about even when consciousness is clouded. I have elsewhere[8] expressed my views about their greater economic significance and the metapsychological reasons for this. These sensations are multilocular, like external perceptions; they may come from different places simultaneously and may thus have different or even opposite qualities.

Sensations of a pleasurable nature have not anything inherently impelling about them, whereas unpleasurable ones have it in the highest degree. The latter impel towards change, towards discharge, and that is why we interpret unpleasure as implying a heightening and pleasure a lowering of energic cathexis.[9] Let us call what becomes conscious as pleasure and unpleasure a quantitative and qualitative 'something' in the course of mental events; the question then is whether this 'something' can become conscious in the place where it is, or whether it must first be transmitted to the system *Pcpt*.

Clinical experience decides for the latter. It shows us that this 'something' behaves like a repressed impulse. It can exert driving force without the ego noticing the compulsion. Not until there is resistance to the compulsion, a hold-up in the discharge-reaction, does the 'something' at once become conscious as unpleasure. In the same way that tensions arising from physical needs can remain unconscious, so also can pain—a thing intermediate between external and internal perception, which behaves like an internal perception even

---

[8][*Beyond the Pleasure Principle* (1920g), *Standard Ed.*, 18, 29; *I.P.L.*, 4, 23.]
[9][Ibid., 8, and ibid., 2.]

when its source is in the external world. It remains true, therefore, that sensations and feelings, too, only become conscious through reaching the system *Pcpt.*; if the way forward is barred, they do not come into being as sensations, although the 'something' that corresponds to them in the course of excitation is the same as if they did. We then come to speak, in a condensed and not entirely correct manner, of 'unconscious feelings', keeping up an analogy with unconscious ideas which is not altogether justifiable. Actually the difference is that, whereas with *Ucs. ideas* connecting links must be created before they can be brought into the *Cs.*, with *feelings*, which are themselves transmitted directly, this does not occur. In other words: the distinction between *Cs.* and *Pcs.* has no meaning where feelings are concerned; the *Pcs.* here drops out—and feelings are either conscious or unconscious. Even when they are attached to word-presentations, their becoming conscious is not due to that circumstance, but they become so directly.[10]

The part played by word-presentations now becomes perfectly clear. By their interposition internal thought-processes are made into perceptions. It is like a demonstration of the theorem that all knowledge has its origin in external perception. When a hypercathexis of the process of thinking takes place, thoughts are *actually* perceived—as if they came from without—and are consequently held to be true.

After this clarifying of the relations between external and internal perception and the superficial system *Pcpt.-Cs.*, we can go on to work out our idea of the ego. It starts out, as we see, from the system *Pcpt.*, which is its nucleus, and begins by embracing the *Pcs.*, which is adjacent to the mnemic residues. But, as we have learnt, the ego is also unconscious.

---

[10][Cf. Section III of 'The Unconscious' (1915*e*), *Standard Ed.*, 14, 177–8.]

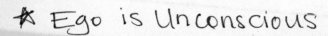

Now I think we shall gain a great deal by following the suggestion of a writer who, from personal motives, vainly asserts that he has nothing to do with the rigours of pure science. I am speaking of Georg Groddeck, who is never tired of insisting that what we call our ego behaves essentially passively in life, and that, as he expresses it, we are 'lived' by unknown and uncontrollable forces.[11] We have all had impressions of the same kind, even though they may not have overwhelmed us to the exclusion of all others, and we need feel no hesitation in finding a place for Groddeck's discovery in the structure of science. I propose to take it into account by calling the entity which starts out from the system *Pcpt.* and begins by being *Pcs.* the 'ego', and by following Groddeck in calling the other part of the mind, into which this entity extends and which behaves as though it were *Ucs.*, the 'id'.[12]

We shall soon see whether we can derive any advantage from this view for purposes either of description or of understanding. We shall now look upon an individual as a psychical id, unknown and unconscious, upon whose surface rests the ego, developed from its nucleus the *Pcpt.* system. If we make an effort to represent this pictorially, we may add that the ego does not completely envelop the id, but only does so to the extent to which the system *Pcpt.* forms its [the ego's] surface, more or less as the germinal disc rests upon the ovum. The ego is not sharply separated from the id; its lower portion merges into it.

But the repressed merges into the id as well, and is merely a part of it. The repressed is only cut off sharply from the

---

[11]Groddeck (1923).

[12][See Editor's Introduction, p. xxxii.]—Groddeck himself no doubt followed the example of Nietzsche, who habitually used this grammatical term for whatever in our nature is impersonal and, so to speak, subject to natural law.

ego by the resistances of repression; it can communicate with the ego through the id. We at once realize that almost all the lines of demarcation we have drawn at the instigation of pathology relate only to the superficial strata of the mental apparatus—the only ones known to us. The state of things which we have been describing can be represented diagrammatically (Fig. 1);[13] though it must be remarked that the form chosen has no pretensions to any special applicability, but is merely intended to serve for purposes of exposition.

We might add, perhaps, that the ego wears a 'cap of hearing'[14]—on one side only, as we learn from cerebral anatomy. It might be said to wear it awry.

It is easy to see that the ego is that part of the id which has been modified by the direct influence of the external

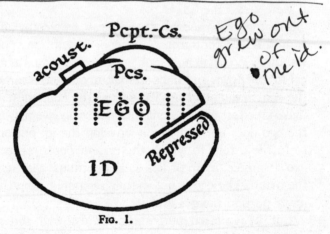

FIG. 1.

---

[13][Compare the slightly different diagram near the end of Lecture XXXI of the *New Introductory Lectures* (1933*a*). The entirely different one in *The Interpretation of Dreams* (1900*a*), *Standard Ed.*, 5, 541, and its predecessor in a letter to Fliess of December 6, 1896 (Freud, 1950*a*, Letter 52), are concerned with function as well as structure.]

[14]['*Hörkappe.*' I.e. the auditory lobe. Cf. footnote 6, p. 13 above.]

world through the medium of the *Pcpt.-Cs.*; in a sense it is an extension of the surface-differentiation. Moreover, the ego seeks to bring the influence of the external world to bear upon the id and its tendencies, and endeavours to substitute the reality principle for the pleasure principle which reigns unrestrictedly in the id. For the ego, perception plays the part which in the id falls to instinct. The ego represents what may be called reason and common sense, in contrast to the id, which contains the passions. All this falls into line with popular distinctions which we are all familiar with; at the same time, however, it is only to be regarded as holding good on the average or 'ideally'.

The functional importance of the ego is manifested in the fact that normally control over the approaches to motility devolves upon it. Thus in its relation to the id it is like a man on horseback, who has to hold in check the superior strength of the horse; with this difference, that the rider tries to do so with his own strength while the ego uses borrowed forces. The analogy may be carried a little further. Often a rider, if he is not to be parted from his horse, is obliged to guide it where it wants to go;[15] so in the same way the ego is in the habit of transforming the id's will into action as if it were its own.

Another factor, besides the influence of the system *Pcpt*, seems to have played a part in bringing about the formation of the ego and its differentiation from the id. A person's own body, and above all its surface, is a place from which both external and internal perceptions may spring. It is *seen* like any other object, but to the *touch* it yields two kinds of sensations, one of which may be equivalent to an internal perception. Psycho-physiology has fully discussed the man-

---

[15][This analogy appears as an association to one of Freud's dreams in *The Interpretation of Dreams, Standard Ed.*, 4, 231.]

ner in which a person's own body attains its special position among other objects in the world of perception. Pain, too, seems to play a part in the process, and the way in which we gain new knowledge of our organs during painful illnesses is perhaps a model of the way by which in general we arrive at the idea of our body.

The ego is first and foremost a bodily ego; it is not merely a surface entity, but is itself the projection of a surface.[16] If we wish to find an anatomical analogy for it we can best identify it with the 'cortical homunculus' of the anatomists, which stands on its head in the cortex, sticks up its heels, faces backwards and, as we know, has its speech-area on the left-hand side.

The relation of the ego to consciousness has been entered into repeatedly; yet there are some important facts in this connection which remain to be described here. Accustomed as we are to taking our social or ethical scale of values along with us wherever we go, we feel no surprise at hearing that the scene of the activities of the lower passions is in the unconscious; we expect, moreover, that the higher any mental function ranks in our scale of values the more easily it will find access to consciousness assured to it. Here, however, psycho-analytic experience disappoints us. On the one hand, we have evidence that even subtle and difficult intellectual operations which ordinarily require strenuous reflection can equally be carried out preconsciously and without coming into consciousness. Instances of this are quite incontestable;

---

[16][I.e. the ego is ultimately derived from bodily sensations, chiefly from those springing from the surface of the body. It may thus be regarded as a mental projection of the surface of the body, besides, as we have seen above, representing the superficies of the mental apparatus.—This footnote first appeared in the English translation of 1927, in which it was described as having been authorized by Freud. It does not appear in the German editions.]

they may occur, for example, during the state of sleep, as is shown when someone finds, immediately after waking, that he knows the solution to a difficult mathematical or other problem with which he had been wrestling in vain the day before.[17]

There is another phenomenon, however, which is far stranger. In our analyses we discover that there are people in whom the faculties of self-criticism and conscience— mental activities, that is, that rank as extremely high ones— are unconscious and unconsciously produce effects of the greatest importance; the example of resistance remaining unconscious during analysis is therefore by no means unique. But this new discovery, which compels us, in spite of our better critical judgment, to speak of an 'unconscious sense of guilt',[18] bewilders us far more than the other and sets us fresh problems, especially when we gradually come to see that in a great number of neuroses an unconscious sense of guilt of this kind plays a decisive economic part and puts the most powerful obstacles in the way of recovery.[19] If we come back once more to our scale of values, we shall have to say that not only what is lowest but also what is highest in the ego can be unconscious. It is as if we were thus supplied with a proof of what we have just asserted of the conscious ego: that it is first and foremost a body-ego.

✱ Body-ego.

---

[17] I was quite recently told an instance of this which was, in fact, brought up as an objection against my description of the 'dream-work'. [Cf. *The Interpretation of Dreams, Standard Ed.*, 4, 64, and 5, 564.]

[18] [This phrase had already appeared in Freud's paper on 'Obsessive Actions and Religious Practices' (1907*b*), *Standard Ed.*, 9, 123. The notion was, however, foreshadowed much earlier, in Section II of the first paper on 'The Neuro-Psychoses of Defence' (1894*a*).]

[19] [This is further discussed below, p. 50 ff.]

III

The Ego and the Super-Ego (Ego Ideal)

If the ego were merely the part of the id modified by the influence of the perceptual system, the representative in the mind of the real external world, we should have a simple state of things to deal with. But there is a further complication.

The considerations that led us to assume the existence of a grade in the ego, a differentiation within the ego, which may be called the 'ego ideal' or 'super-ego', have been stated elsewhere.[1] They still hold good.[2] The fact that this part of the ego is less firmly connected with consciousness is the novelty which calls for explanation.

---

[1] [See Editor's Introd., pp. xxxv–xxxvi.] Cf. 'On Narcissism: an Introduction' (1914c), and *Group Psychology and the Analysis of the Ego* (1921c).
[2] Except that I seem to have been mistaken in ascribing the function of 'reality-testing' to this super-ego—a point which needs correction. [See 1921c, *S.E.*, 18, 114 and *n.* 2; *I.P.L.*, 6, 46 and *n.* 2, and the Editor's Note to the metapsychological paper on dreams (1917d), 14, 220.] It would fit in perfectly with the relations of the ego to the world of perception if reality-testing remained a task of the ego itself. Some earlier suggestions about a 'nucleus of the ego', never very definitely formulated, also require to be put right, since the system *Pcpt.-Cs.* alone can be regarded as the nucleus of the ego. [In *Beyond the Pleasure Principle* (1920g) Freud had spoken of the unconscious part of the ego as its nucleus (*S.E.*, 18, 19; *I.P.L.*, 4, 13); and in his later paper on 'Humour' (1927d) he referred to the super-ego as the nucleus of the ego.]

At this point we must widen our range a little. We succeeded in explaining the painful disorder of melancholia by
supposing that [in those suffering from it] an object which
was lost has been set up again inside the ego—that is, that
an object-cathexis has been replaced by an identification.[3]
At that time, however, we did not appreciate the full significance of this process and did not know how common and
how typical it is. Since then we have come to understand
that this kind of substitution has a great share in determin-
ing the form taken by the ego and that it makes an essential
contribution towards building up what is called its 'character'.[4]

At the very beginning, in the individual's primitive oral
phase, object-cathexis and identification are no doubt indis-
tinguishable from each other.[5] We can only suppose that
later on object-cathexes proceed from the id, which feels
erotic trends as needs. The ego, which to begin with is still
feeble, becomes aware of the object-cathexes, and either
acquiesces in them or tries to fend them off by the process
of repression.[6]

When it happens that a person has to give up a sexual
object, there quite often ensues an alteration of his ego

---

[3]'Mourning and Melancholia' (1917e) [*Standard Ed.*, 14, 249].
[4][Some references to other passages in which Freud has discussed charac-
ter-formation will be found in an Editor's footnote at the end of the paper
on 'Character and Anal Erotism' (1908b), *Standard Ed.*, 9, 175.]
[5][Cf. Chap. VII of *Group Psychology* (1921c), S.E., 18, 105; I.P.L., 6, 37.]
[6]An interesting parallel to the replacement of object-choice by identification is to be found in the belief of primitive peoples, and in the prohibitions
based upon it, that the attributes of animals which are incorporated as
nourishment persist as part of the character of those who eat them. As is
well known, this belief is one of the roots of cannibalism and its effects have
continued through the series of usages of the totem meal down to Holy
Communion. [Cf. *Totem and Taboo* (1912–13), *Standard Ed.*, 13, 82, 142,
154–5, etc.] The consequences ascribed by this belief to oral mastery of the
object do in fact follow in the case of the later sexual object-choice.

which can only be described as a setting up of the object inside the ego, as it occurs in melancholia; the exact nature of this substitution is as yet unknown to us. It may be that this introjection, which is a kind of regression to the mechanism of the oral phase, the ego makes it easier for the object to be given up or renders that process possible. It may be that this identification is the sole condition under which the id can give up its objects. At any rate the process, especially in the early phases of development, is a very frequent one, and it makes it possible to suppose that the character of the ego is a precipitate of abandoned object-cathexes and that it contains the history of those object-choices. It must, of course, be admitted from the outset that there are varying degrees of capacity for resistance, which decide the extent to which a person's character fends off or accepts the influences of the history of his erotic object-choices. In women who have had many experiences in love there seems to be no difficulty in finding vestiges of their object-cathexes in the traits of their character. We must also take into consideration cases of simultaneous object-cathexis and identification—cases, that is, in which the alteration in character occurs before the object has been given up. In such cases the alteration in character has been able to survive the object-relation and in a certain sense to conserve it.

From another point of view it may be said that this transformation of an erotic object-choice into an alteration of the ego is also a method by which the ego can obtain control over the id and deepen its relations with it—at the cost, it is true, of acquiescing to a large extent in the id's experiences. When the ego assumes the features of the object, it is forcing itself, so to speak, upon the id as a love-object and is trying to make good the id's loss by saying: 'Look, you can love me too—I am so like the object.'

The transformation of object-libido into narcissistic libido which thus takes place obviously implies an abandonment of sexual aims, a desexualization—a kind of sublimation, therefore. Indeed, the question arises, and deserves careful consideration, whether this is not the universal road to sublimation, whether all sublimation does not take place through the mediation of the ego, which begins by changing sexual object-libido into narcissistic libido and then, perhaps, goes on to give it another aim.[7] We shall later on have to consider whether other instinctual vicissitudes may not also result from this transformation, whether, for instance, it may not bring about a defusion of the various instincts that are fused together.[8]

Although it is a digression from our aim, we cannot avoid giving our attention for a moment longer to the ego's object-identifications. If they obtain the upper hand and become too numerous, unduly powerful and incompatible with one another, a pathological outcome will not be far off. It may come to a disruption of the ego in consequence of the different identifications becoming cut off from one another by resistances; perhaps the secret of the cases of what is described as 'multiple personality' is that the different identifications seize hold of consciousness in turn. Even when things do not go so far as this, there remains the question of conflicts between the various identifications into which the ego comes apart, conflicts which cannot after all be described as entirely pathological.

---

[7] Now that we have distinguished between the ego and the id, we must recognize the id as the great reservoir of libido indicated in my paper on narcissism (1914c) [*Standard Ed.*, 14, 75]. The libido which flows into the ego owing to the identifications described above brings about its 'secondary narcissism'. [The point is elaborated below on p. 45.]

[8] [Freud returns to the subject of this paragraph below, on pp. 44 and 56. The concept of the fusion and defusion of instincts is explained on pp. 31–2. The terms had been introduced already in an encyclopaedia article (1923a), *Standard Ed.*, 18, 258.]

Identification with father (handwritten margin note)

But, whatever the character's later capacity for resisting the influences of abandoned object-cathexes may turn out to be, the effects of the first identifications made in earliest childhood will be general and lasting. This leads us back to the origin of the ego ideal; for behind it there lies hidden an individual's first and most important identification, his identification with the father in his own personal prehistory.[9] This is apparently not in the first instance the consequence or outcome of an object-cathexis; it is a direct and immediate identification and takes place earlier than any object-cathexis.[10] But the object-choices belonging to the first sexual period and relating to the father and mother seem normally to find their outcome in an identification of this kind, and would thus reinforce the primary one.

The whole subject, however, is so complicated that it will be necessary to go into it in greater detail. The intricacy of the problem is due to two factors: the triangular character of the Oedipus situation and the constitutional bisexuality of each individual.

In its simplified form the case of a male child may be described as follows. At a very early age the little boy develops an object-cathexis for his mother, which originally related to the mother's breast and is the prototype of an

---

[9]Perhaps it would be safer to say 'with the parents'; for before a child has arrived at definite knowledge of the difference between the sexes, the lack of a penis, it does not distinguish in value between its father and its mother. I recently came across the instance of a young married woman whose story showed that, after noticing the lack of a penis in herself, she had supposed it to be absent not in all women, but only in those whom she regarded as inferior, and had still supposed that her mother possessed one. [Cf. a footnote to 'The Infantile Genital Organization' (1923e), S.E., 19, 145.]— In order to simplify my presentation I shall discuss only identification with the father.

[10][See the beginning of Chapter VII of *Group Psychology* (1921c), *Standard Ed.*, 18, 105; *I.P.L.*, 6, 37.]

object-choice on the anaclitic model;[11] the boy deals with his father by identifying himself with him. For a time these two relationships proceed side by side, until the boy's sexual wishes in regard to his mother become more intense and his father is perceived as an obstacle to them; from this the Oedipus complex originates.[12] His identification with his father then takes on a hostile colouring and changes into a wish to get rid of his father in order to take his place with his mother. Henceforward his relation to his father is ambivalent; it seems as if the ambivalence inherent in the identification from the beginning had become manifest. An ambivalent attitude to his father and an object-relation of a solely affectionate kind to his mother make up the content of the simple positive Oedipus complex in a boy.

Along with the demolition of the Oedipus complex, the boy's object-cathexis of his mother must be given up. Its place may be filled by one of two things: either an identification with his mother or an intensification of his identification with his father. We are accustomed to regard the latter outcome as the more normal; it permits the affectionate relation to the mother to be in a measure retained. In this way the dissolution of the Oedipus complex[13] would consolidate the masculinity in a boy's character. In a precisely analogous way,[14] the outcome of the Oedipus attitude in a little girl may be an intensification of her identification with her mother (or the setting up of such an identification

---

[11][See the paper on narcissism (1914c), *Standard Ed.*, 14, 87 ff.]
[12]Cf. *Group Psychology* (1921c), loc. cit.
[13][Cf. the paper bearing this title (1924d) in which Freud discussed the question more fully.]
[14][The idea that the outcome of the Oedipus complex was 'precisely analogous' in girls and boys was abandoned by Freud not long after this. See 'Some Psychical Consequences of the Anatomical Distinction between the Sexes' (1925j).]

for the first time)—a result which will fix the child's feminine character.

These identifications are not what we should have expected [from the previous account (p. 24)], since they do not
introduce the abandoned object into the ego; but this alternative outcome may also occur, and is easier to observe in
girls than in boys. Analysis very often shows that a little girl,
after she has had to relinquish her father as a love-object, will
bring her masculinity into prominence and identify herself
with her father (that is, with the object which has been lost),
instead of with her mother. This will clearly depend on
whether the masculinity in her disposition—whatever that
may consist in—is strong enough.

tomboy

It would appear, therefore, that in both sexes the relative
strength of the masculine and feminine sexual dispositions
is what determines whether the outcome of the Oedipus
situation shall be an identification with the father or with
the mother. This is one of the ways in which bisexuality
takes a hand in the subsequent vicissitudes of the Oedipus
complex. The other way is even more important. For one
gets an impression that the simple Oedipus complex is by
no means its commonest form, but rather represents a simplification or schematization which, to be sure, is often
enough justified for practical purposes. Closer study usually
discloses the more complete Oedipus complex, which is
twofold, positive and negative, and is due to the bisexuality
originally present in children: that is to say, a boy has not
merely an ambivalent attitude towards his father and an
affectionate object-choice towards his mother, but at the
same time he also behaves like a girl and displays an affectionate feminine attitude to his father and a corresponding
jealousy and hostility towards his mother. It is this complicating element introduced by bisexuality that makes it so
difficult to obtain a clear view of the facts in connection with

the earliest object-choices and identifications, and still more difficult to describe them intelligibly. It may even be that the ambivalence displayed in the relations to the parents should be attributed entirely to bisexuality and that it is not, as I have represented above, developed out of identification in consequence of rivalry.[15]

In my opinion it is advisable in general, and quite especially where neurotics are concerned, to assume the existence of the complete Oedipus complex. Analytic experience then shows that in a number of cases one or the other constituent disappears, except for barely distinguishable traces; so that the result is a series with the normal positive Oedipus complex at one end and the inverted negative one at the other, while its intermediate members exhibit the complete form with one or other of its two components preponderating. At the dissolution of the Oedipus complex the four trends of which it consists will group themselves in such a way as to produce a father-identification and a mother-identification. The father-identification will preserve the object-relation to the mother which belonged to the positive complex and will at the same time replace the object-relation to the father which belonged to the inverted complex: and the same will be true, *mutatis mutandis*, of the mother-identification. The relative intensity of the two identifications in any individual will reflect the preponder-

---

[15][Freud's belief in the importance of bisexuality went back a very long way. In the first edition of the *Three Essays* (1905d), for instance, he wrote: 'Without taking bisexuality into account I think it would scarcely be possible to arrive at an understanding of the sexual manifestations that are actually to be observed in men and women.' (*S.E.*, 7, 220; *I.P.L.*, 57, 86.) Still earlier we find a passage in a letter to Fliess (who influenced him greatly on this subject) which seems almost to foreshadow the present paragraph (Freud, 1950a, Letter 113, of August 1, 1899): 'Bisexuality! I am sure you are right about it. And I am accustoming myself to regarding every sexual act as an event between four individuals.']

ance in him of one or other of the two sexual dispositions.

The broad general outcome of the sexual phase dominated by the Oedipus complex may, therefore, be taken to be the forming of a precipitate in the ego, consisting of these two identifications in some way united with each other. This modification of the ego retains its special position; it confronts the other contents of the ego as an ego ideal or super-ego.

The super-ego is, however, not simply a residue of the earliest object-choices of the id; it also represents an energetic reaction-formation against those choices. Its relation to the ego is not exhausted by the precept: 'You *ought to be* like this (like your father).' It also comprises the prohibition: 'You *may not be* like this (like your father)—that is, you may not do all that he does; some things are his prerogative.' This double aspect of the ego ideal derives from the fact that the ego ideal had the task of repressing the Oedipus complex; indeed, it is to that revolutionary event that it owes its existence. Clearly the repression of the Oedipus complex was no easy task. The child's parents, and especially his father, were perceived as the obstacle to a realization of his Oedipus wishes; so his infantile ego fortified itself for the carrying out of the repression by erecting this same obstacle within itself. It borrowed strength to do this. so to speak, from the father, and this loan was an extraordinarily momentous act. The super-ego retains the character of the father, while the more powerful the Oedipus complex was and the more rapidly it succumbed to repression (under the influence of authority, religious teaching, schooling and reading), the stricter will be the domination of the super-ego over the ego later on—in the form of conscience or perhaps of an unconscious sense of guilt. I shall presently [pp. 48–49] bring forward a suggestion about the source of its power to dominate in this way—the source, that is, of its compulsive character which manifests itself in the form of a categorical imperative.

If we consider once more the origin of the super-ego as we have described it, we shall recognize that it is the outcome of two highly important factors, one of a biological and the other of a historical nature: namely, the lengthy duration in man of his childhood helplessness and dependence, and the fact of his Oedipus complex, the repression of which we have shown to be connected with the interruption of libidinal development by the latency period and so with the diphasic onset of man's sexual life.[16] According to one psycho-analytic hypothesis,[17] the last-mentioned phenomenon, which seems to be peculiar to man, is a heritage of the cultural development necessitated by the glacial epoch. We see, then, that the differentiation of the super-ego from the ego is no matter of chance; it represents the most important characteristics of the development both of the individual and of the species; indeed, by giving permanent expression to the influence of the parents it perpetuates the existence of the factors to which it owes its origin.

Psycho-analysis has been reproached time after time with ignoring the higher, moral, supra-personal side of human nature. The reproach is doubly unjust, both historically and

---

[16][In the German editions this sentence reads as follows: 'If we consider once more the origin of the super-ego as we have described it, we shall recognize that it is the outcome of two highly important biological factors: namely, the lengthy duration in man of his childhood helplessness and dependence, and the fact of his Oedipus complex, which we have traced back to the interruption of libidinal development by the latency period and so to the diphasic origin of man's sexual life.' The slightly different version given in the text above was inserted by Freud's express orders in the English translation in 1927. For some reason the emendations were not included in the later German editions.]

[17][The idea was put forward by Ferenczi (1913). Freud seems to accept it rather more definitely near the end of Chapter X of *Inhibitions, Symptoms and Anxiety* (1926d), *Standard Ed.*, 20, 155; *I.P.L.*, 28, 69.]

methodologically. For, in the first place, we have from the very beginning attributed the function of instigating repression to the moral and aesthetic trends in the ego, and secondly, there has been a general refusal to recognize that psycho-analytic research could not, like a philosophical system, produce a complete and ready-made theoretical structure, but had to find its way step by step along the path towards understanding the intricacies of the mind by making an analytic dissection of both normal and abnormal phenomena. So long as we had to concern ourselves with the study of what is repressed in mental life, there was no need for us to share in any agitated apprehensions as to the whereabouts of the higher side of man. But now that we have embarked upon the analysis of the ego we can give an answer to all those whose moral sense has been shocked and who have complained that there must surely be a higher nature in man: 'Very true,' we can say, 'and here we have that higher nature, in this ego ideal or super-ego, the representative of our relation to our parents. When we were little children we knew these higher natures, we admired them and feared them; and later we took them into ourselves.'

The ego ideal is therefore the heir of the Oedipus complex, and thus it is also the expression of the most powerful impulses and most important libidinal vicissitudes of the id. By setting up this ego ideal, the ego has mastered the Oedipus complex and at the same time placed itself in subjection to the id. Whereas the ego is essentially the representative of the external world, of reality, the super-ego stands in contrast to it as the representative of the internal world, of the id. Conflicts between the ego and the ideal will, as we are now prepared to find, ultimately reflect the contrast between what is real and what is psychical, between the external world and the internal world.

Through the forming of the ideal, what biology and the

vicissitudes of the human species have created in the id and left behind in it is taken over by the ego and re experienced in relation to itself as an individual. Owing to the way in which the ego ideal is formed, it has the most abundant links with the phylogenetic acquisition of each individual—his archaic heritage. What has belonged to the lowest part of the mental life of each of us is changed, through the formation of the ideal, into what is highest in the human mind by our scale of values. It would be vain, however, to attempt to localize the ego ideal, even in the sense in which we have localized the ego,[18] or to work it into any of the analogies with the help of which we have tried to picture the relation between the ego and the id.

It is easy to show that the ego ideal answers to everything that is expected of the higher nature of man. As a substitute for a longing for the father, it contains the germ from which all religions have evolved. The self-judgement which declares that the ego falls short of its ideal produces the religious sense of humility to which the believer appeals in his longing. As a child grows up, the role of father is carried on by teachers and others in authority; their injunctions and prohibitions remain powerful in the ego ideal and continue, in the form of conscience, to exercise the moral censorship. The tension between the demands of conscience and the actual performances of the ego is experienced as a sense of guilt. Social feelings rest on identifications with other people, on the basis of having the same ego ideal.

Religion, morality, and a social sense—the chief elements in the higher side of man[19]—were originally one and the same thing. According to the hypothesis which I put for-

---

[18][The super-ego is accordingly not included in the diagram on p. 18. Nevertheless it is given a place in the later diagram in Lecture XXXI of the *New Introductory Lectures* (1933a).]

[19]I am at the moment putting science and art on one side.

ward in *Totem and Taboo*[20] they were acquired
phylogenetically out of the father-complex: religion and
moral restraint through the process of mastering the Oedipus complex itself, and social feeling through the necessity
for overcoming the rivalry that then remained between the
members of the younger generation. The male sex seems to
have taken the lead in all these moral acquisitions; and they
seem to have then been transmitted to women by cross-
inheritance. Even to-day the social feelings arise in the individual as a superstructure built upon impulses of jealous
rivalry against his brothers and sisters. Since the hostility
cannot be satisfied, an identification with the former rival
develops. The study of mild cases of homosexuality confirms
the suspicion that in this instance, too, the identification is
a substitute for an affectionate object-choice which has
taken the place of the aggressive, hostile attitude.[21]

With the mention of phylogenesis, however, fresh problems arise, from which one is tempted to draw cautiously
back. But there is no help for it, the attempt must be
made—in spite of a fear that it will lay bare the inadequacy
of our whole effort. The question is: which was it, the ego
of primitive man or his id, that acquired religion and morality in those early days out of the father-complex? If it was
his ego, why do we not speak simply of these things being
inherited by the ego? If it was the id, how does that agree
with the character of the id? Or are we wrong in carrying
the differentiation between ego, super-ego, and id back into
such early times? Or should we not honestly confess that our
whole conception of the processes in the ego is of no help
in understanding phylogenesis and cannot be applied to it?

---

[20][Freud (1912–13), *Standard Ed.*, **13**, 146 ff.]
[21]Cf. *Group Psychology* (1921*c*) [*S.E.*, **18**, 120; *I.P.L.*, **6**, 52] and 'Some
Neurotic Mechanisms in Jealousy, Paranoia and Homosexuality' (1922*b*)
[*Standard Ed.*, **18**, 231].

Let us answer first what is easiest to answer. The differentiation between ego and id must be attributed not only to primitive man but even to much simpler organisms, for it is the inevitable expression of the influence of the external world. The super-ego, according to our hypothesis, actually originated from the experiences that led to totemism. The question whether it was the ego or the id that experienced and acquired these things soon comes to nothing. Reflection at once shows us that no external vicissitudes can be experienced or undergone by the id, except by way of the ego, which is the representative of the external world to the id. Nevertheless it is not possible to speak of direct inheritance in the ego. It is here that the gulf between an actual individual and the concept of a species becomes evident. Moreover, one must not take the difference between ego and id in too hard-and-fast a sense, nor forget that the ego is a specially differentiated part of the id [p. 19]. The experiences of the ego seem at first to be lost for inheritance; but, when they have been repeated often enough and with sufficient strength in many individuals in successive generations, they transform themselves, so to say, into experiences of the id, the impressions of which are preserved by heredity. Thus in the id, which is capable of being inherited, are harboured residues of the existences of countless egos; and, when the ego forms its super-ego out of the id, it may perhaps only be reviving shapes of former egos and be bringing them to resurrection.

The way in which the super-ego came into being explains how it is that the early conflicts of the ego with the object-cathexes of the id can be continued in conflicts with their heir, the super-ego. If the ego has not succeeded in properly mastering the Oedipus complex, the energic cathexis of the latter, springing from the id, will come into operation once more in the reaction-formation of the ego ideal. The abundant communication between the ideal and these *Ucs.* instinctual impulses solves the puzzle of how it is that the ideal itself can to a great extent remain unconscious and inaccessible to the ego. The struggle which once raged in the deepest strata of the mind, and was not brought to an end by rapid sublimation and identification, is now continued in a higher region, like the Battle of the Huns in Kaulbach's painting.[22]

---

[22][This was the battle, usually known as the Battle of Châlons, in which, in 451, Attila was defeated by the Romans and Visigoths. Wilhelm von Kaulbach (1805–1874) made it the subject of one of his mural decorations, originally painted for the Neues Museum in Berlin. In this the dead warriors are represented as continuing their fight in the sky above the battlefield, in accordance with a legend that can be traced back to the fifth century Neo-Platonist, Damascius.]

IV

The Two Classes of Instincts

We have already said that, if the differentiation we have made of the mind into an id, an ego, and a super-ego represents any advance in our knowledge, it ought to enable us to understand more thoroughly the dynamic relations within the mind and to describe them more clearly. We have also already concluded [p. 19] that the ego is especially under the influence of perception, and that, speaking broadly, perceptions may be said to have the same significance for the ego as instincts have for the id. At the same time the ego is subject to the influence of the instincts, too, like the id, of which it is, as we know, only a specially modified part.

I have lately developed a view of the instincts[1] which I shall here hold to and take as the basis of my further discussions. According to this view we have to distinguish two classes of instincts, one of which, the sexual instincts or Eros, is by far the more conspicuous and accessible to study. It comprises not merely the uninhibited sexual instinct proper and the instinctual impulses of an aim-inhibited or sublimated nature derived from it, but also the self-preservative instinct, which must be assigned to the ego and which at the beginning of our analytic work we had good reason

---

[1]*Beyond the Pleasure Principle* [1920g].

Ego is under the influence of perception.

for contrasting with the sexual object-instincts. The second class of instincts was not so easy to point to; in the end we came to recognize sadism as its representative. On the basis of theoretical considerations, supported by biology, we put forward the hypothesis of a death instinct, the task of which is to lead organic life back into the inanimate state; on the other hand, we supposed that Eros, by bringing about a more and more far-reaching combination of the particles into which living substance is dispersed, aims at complicating life and at the same time, of course, at preserving it. Acting in this way, both the instincts would be conservative in the strictest sense of the word, since both would be endeavouring to re-establish a state of things that was disturbed by the emergence of life. The emergence of life would thus be the cause of the continuance of life and also at the same time of the striving towards death; and life itself would be a conflict and compromise between these two trends. The problem of the origin of life would remain a cosmological one; and the problem of the goal and purpose of life would be answered dualistically[2]

On this view, a special physiological process (of anabolism or catabolism) would be associated with each of the two classes of instincts; both kinds of instinct would be active in every particle of living substance, though in unequal proportions, so that some one substance might be the principal representative of Eros.

This hypothesis throws no light whatever upon the manner in which the two classes of instincts are fused, blended, and alloyed with each other; but that this takes place regularly and very extensively is an assumption indispensable to our conception. It appears that, as a result of the combination of unicellular organisms into multicellular forms of life,

---

[2][Cf. footnote 11, p. 45 below.]

the death instinct of the single cell can successfully be neu-
tralized and the destructive impulses be diverted on to the
external world through the instrumentality of a special
organ. This special organ would seem to be the muscular
apparatus; and the death instinct would thus seem to express
itself—though probably only in part—as an instinct of destruction directed against the external world and other organisms.[3]

Once we have admitted the idea of a fusion of the two
classes of instincts with each other, the possibility of
a—more or less complete—'defusion' of them forces itself
upon us.[4] The sadistic component of the sexual instinct
would be a classical example of a serviceable instinctual
fusion; and the sadism which has made itself independent
as a perversion would be typical of a defusion, though not
of one carried to extremes. From this point we obtain a view
of a great domain of facts which has not before been considered in this light. We perceive that for purposes of discharge
the instinct of destruction is habitually brought into the
service of Eros; we suspect that the epileptic fit is a product
and indication of an instinctual defusion;[5] and we come to
understand that instinctual defusion and the marked emergence of the death instinct call for particular consideration
among the effects of some severe neuroses—for instance,
the obsessional neuroses. Making a swift generalization, we
might conjecture that the essence of a regression of libido
(e.g. from the genital to the sadistic-anal phase) lies in a
defusion of instincts, just as, conversely, the advance from
the earlier phase to the definitive genital one would be

---

[3][Freud returns to this in 'The Economic Problem of Masochism', *S.E.*, 19, 163].

[4][Cf. above, p. 25. What follows in regard to sadism is hinted at in *Beyond the Pleasure Principle* (1920g) *S.E.*, 18, 54; *I.P.L.*, 4, 48.]

[5][Cf. Freud's later paper on Dostoevsky's fits (1928b).]

conditioned by an accession of erotic components.[6] The
question also arises whether ordinary ambivalence, which is
so often unusually strong in the constitutional disposition to
neurosis, should not be regarded as the product of a defusion; ambivalence, however, is such a fundamental phenomenon that it more probably represents an instinctual fusion
that has not been completed.

It is natural that we should turn with interest to enquire
whether there may not be instructive connections to be
traced between the structures we have assumed to exist—
the ego, the super-ego and the id—on the one hand and the
two classes of instincts on the other; and, further, whether
the pleasure principle which dominates mental processes
can be shown to have any constant relation both to the two
classes of instincts and to these differentiations which we
have drawn in the mind. But before we discuss this, we must
clear away a doubt which arises concerning the terms in
which the problem itself is stated. There is, it is true, no
doubt about the pleasure principle, and the differentiation
within the ego has good clinical justification; but the distinction between the two classes of instincts does not seem
sufficiently assured and it is possible that facts of clinical
analysis may be found which will do away with its preten-
sion.

One such fact there appears to be. For the opposition
between the two classes of instincts we may put the polarity
of love and hate.[7] There is no difficulty in finding a representative of Eros; but we must be grateful that we can find

---

[6][Freud recurs to this point in *Inhibitions, Symptoms and Anxiety* (1926d),
Standard Ed., **20**, 114; *I.P.L.*, **28**, 28.]
[7][For what follows, see the earlier discussion of the relation between love
and hate in 'Instincts and their Vicissitudes' (1915c), *Standard Ed.*, **14**,
136–40, as well as the later one in Chapters V and VI of *Civilization and
its Discontents* (1930a).]

a representative of the elusive death instinct in the instinct of destruction, to which hate points the way. Now, clinical observation shows not only that love is with unexpected regularity accompanied by hate (ambivalence), and not only that in human relationships hate is frequently a forerunner of love, but also that in a number of circumstances hate changes into love and love into hate. If this change is more than a mere succession in time—if, that is, one of them actually turns into the other—then clearly the ground is cut away from under a distinction so fundamental as that between erotic instincts and death instincts, one which presupposes physiological processes running in opposite directions.

Now the case in which someone first loves and then hates the same person (or the reverse) because that person has given him cause for doing so, has obviously nothing to do with our problem. Nor has the other case, in which feelings of love that have not yet become manifest express themselves to begin with by hostility and aggressive tendencies; for it may be that here the destructive component in the object-cathexis has hurried on ahead and is only later on joined by the erotic one. But we know of several instances in the psychology of the neuroses in which it is more plausible to suppose that a transformation does take place. In persecutory paranoia the patient fends off an excessively strong homosexual attachment to some particular person in a special way; and as a result this person whom he loved most becomes a persecutor, against whom the patient directs an often dangerous aggressiveness. Here we have a right to interpolate a previous phase which has transformed the love into hate. In the case of the origin of homosexuality, and of desexualized social feelings as well, analytic investigation has only recently taught us to recognize that violent feelings of rivalry are present which lead to aggressive inclinations, and that it is only after these have been surmounted that the formerly hated object becomes the loved one or gives rise to an identification.[8] The question arises whether in these instances we are to assume a direct transformation of hate into love. It is clear that here the changes are purely internal and an alteration in the behaviour of the object plays no part in them.

There is another possible mechanism, however, which we have come to know of by analytic investigation of the processes concerned in the change in paranoia. An ambivalent attitude is present from the outset and the transformation is effected by means of a reactive displacement of cathexis, energy being withdrawn from the erotic impulse and added to the hostile one.

Not quite the same thing but something like it happens when the hostile rivalry leading to homosexuality is overcome. The hostile attitude has no prospect of satisfaction; consequently—for economic reasons, that is—it is replaced by a loving attitude for which there is more prospect of satisfaction—that is, possibility of discharge. So we see that we are not obliged in any of these cases to assume a direct transformation of hate into love, which would be incompatible with the qualitative distinction between the two classes of instincts.

It will be noticed, however, that by introducing this other mechanism of changing love into hate, we have tacitly made another assumption which deserves to be stated explicitly. We have reckoned as though there existed in the mind—whether in the ego or in the id—a displaceable energy, which, neutral in itself, can be added to a qualitatively differentiated erotic or destructive impulse, and augment its total cathexis. Without assuming the existence of a displaceable energy of this kind we can make no headway. The only

---

[8][See footnote 21, p. 34.]

question is where it comes from, what it belongs to, and what it signifies.

The problem of the quality of instinctual impulses and of its persistence throughout their various vicissitudes is still very obscure and has hardly been attacked up to the present. In the sexual component instincts, which are especially accessible to observation, it is possible to perceive a few processes which are in the same category as what we are discussing. We see, for instance, that some degree of communication exists between the component instincts, that an instinct deriving from one particular erotogenic source can make over its intensity to reinforce another component instinct originating from another source, that the satisfaction of one instinct can take the place of the satisfaction of another, and more facts of the same nature—which must encourage us to venture upon certain hypotheses.

In the present discussion, moreover, I am only putting forward a hypothesis; I have no proof to offer. It seems a plausible view that this displaceable and neutral energy, which is no doubt active both in the ego and in the id, proceeds from the narcissistic store of libido—that it is desexualized Eros. (The erotic instincts appear to be altogether more plastic, more readily diverted and displaced than the destructive instincts.) From this we can easily go on to assume that this displaceable libido is employed in the service of the pleasure principle to obviate blockages and to facilitate discharge. In this connection it is easy to observe a certain indifference as to the path along which the discharge takes place, so long as it takes place somehow. We know this trait; it is characteristic of the cathectic processes in the id. It is found in erotic cathexes, where a peculiar indifference in regard to the object displays itself; and it is especially evident in the transferences arising in analysis, which develop inevitably, irrespective of the persons who are

displaced
Libido

their object. Not long ago Rank [1913] published some good examples of the way in which neurotic acts of revenge can be directed against the wrong people. Such behaviour on the part of the unconscious reminds one of the comic story of the three village tailors, one of whom had to be hanged because the only village blacksmith had committed a capital offence.[9] Punishment must be exacted even if it does not fall upon the guilty. It was in studying the dream-work that we first came upon this kind of looseness in the displacements brought about by the primary process. In that case it was the objects that were thus relegated to a position of no more than secondary importance, just as in the case we are now discussing it is the paths of discharge. It would be characteristic of the ego to be more particular about the choice both of an object and of a path of discharge.

If this displaceable energy is desexualized libido, it may also be described as *sublimated* energy; for it would still retain the main purpose of Eros—that of uniting and binding—in so far as it helps towards establishing the unity, or tendency to unity, which is particularly characteristic of the ego. If thought-processes in the wider sense are to be included among these displacements, then the activity of thinking is also supplied from the sublimation of erotic motive forces.

Here we arrive again at the possibility which has already been discussed [p. 25] that sublimation may take place regularly through the mediation of the ego. The other case will be recollected, in which the ego deals with the first object-cathexes of the id (and certainly with later ones too) by taking over the libido from them into itself and binding it to the alteration of the ego produced by means of identifica-

---

[9][The story was told by Freud in the last chapter of his book on jokes (1905c), *Standard Ed.*, 8, 206.]

tion. The transformation [of erotic libido] into ego-libido of course involves an abandonment of sexual aims, a desexualization. In any case this throws light upon an important function of the ego in its relation to Eros. By thus getting hold of the libido from the object-cathexes, setting itself up as sole love-object, and desexualizing or sublimating the libido of the id, the ego is working in opposition to the purposes of Eros and placing itself at the service of the opposing instinctual impulses. It has to acquiesce in some of the other object-cathexes of the id; it has, so to speak, to participate in them. We shall come back later to another possible consequence of this activity of the ego [p. 56].

This would seem to imply an important amplification of the theory of narcissism. At the very beginning, all the libido is accumulated in the id, while the ego is still in process of formation or is still feeble. The id sends part of this libido out into erotic object-cathexes, whereupon the ego, now grown stronger, tries to get hold of this object-libido and to force itself on the id as a love-object. The narcissism of the ego is thus a secondary one, which has been withdrawn from objects.[10]

Over and over again we find, when we are able to trace instinctual impulses back, that they reveal themselves as derivatives of Eros. If it were not for the considerations put forward in *Beyond the Pleasure Principle,* and ultimately for the sadistic constituents which have attached themselves to Eros, we should have difficulty in holding to our fundamental dualistic point of view.[11] But since we cannot escape that

---

[10][See Appendix B (p. 67) for a discussion of this.]
[11][The consistency with which Freud held to a dualistic classification of the instincts will be seen from his long footnote at the end of Chapter VI of *Beyond the Pleasure Principle* (1920g), *S.E.,* 18, 60–1, *I.P.L.,* 4, 54–5, and from the historical sketch in the Editor's Note to 'Instincts and their Vicissitudes' (1915c), *Standard Ed.,* 14, 113–16.]

view, we are driven to conclude that the death instincts are by their nature mute and that the clamour of life proceeds for the most part from Eros.[12]

And from the struggle against Eros! It can hardly be doubted that the pleasure principle serves the id as a compass in its struggle against the libido—the force that introduces disturbances into the process of life. If it is true that Fechner's principle of constancy[13] governs life, which thus consists of a continuous descent towards death, it is the claims of Eros, of the sexual instincts, which, in the form of instinctual needs, hold up the falling level and introduce fresh tensions. The id, guided by the pleasure principle—that is, by the perception of unpleasure—fends off these tensions in various ways. It does so in the first place by complying as swiftly as possible with the demands of the non-desexualized libido—by striving for the satisfaction of the directly sexual trends. But it does so in a far more comprehensive fashion in relation to one particular form of satisfaction in which all component demands converge—by discharge of the sexual substances, which are saturated vehicles, so to speak, of the erotic tensions.[14] The ejection of the sexual substances in the sexual act corresponds in a sense to the separation of soma and germ-plasm. This accounts for the likeness of the condition that follows complete sexual satisfaction to dying, and for the fact that death coincides with the act of copulation in some of the lower animals. These creatures die in the act of reproduction because, after

---

[12]In fact, on our view it is through the agency of Eros that the destructive instincts that are directed towards the external world have been diverted from the self.

[13][Cf. *Beyond the Pleasure Principle, S.E.,* 18, 8–10; *I.P.L.,* 4, 2–4.]

[14][Freud's views on the part played by the 'sexual substances' will be found in Section 2 of the third of his *Three Essays* (1905d), *Standard Ed.,* 7, 212–16; *I.P.L.,* 57, 78–82.]

Eros has been eliminated through the process of satisfaction, the death instinct has a free hand for accomplishing its purposes. Finally, as we have seen, the ego, by sublimating some of the libido for itself and its purposes, assists the id in its work of mastering the tensions.

The Dependent Relationships
of the Ego

The complexity of our subject-matter must be an excuse for the fact that none of the chapter-headings of this book quite correspond to their contents, and that in turning to new aspects of the topic we are constantly harking back to matters that have already been dealt with.

Thus we have said repeatedly that the ego is formed to a great extent out of identifications which take the place of abandoned cathexes by the id; that the first of these identifications always behave as a special agency in the ego and stand apart from the ego in the form of a super-ego, while later on, as it grows stronger, the ego may become more resistant to the influences of such identifications. The super-ego owes its special position in the ego, or in relation to the ego, to a factor which must be considered from two sides: on the one hand it was the first identification and one which took place while the ego was still feeble, and on the other hand it is the heir to the Oedipus complex and has thus introduced the most momentous objects into the ego. The super-ego's relation to the later alterations of the ego is roughly similar to that of the primary sexual phase of childhood to later sexual life after puberty. Although it is accessible to all later influences, it nevertheless preserves throughout life the character given to it by its derivation from the

[handwritten margin note: How the ego is formed]

father-complex—namely, the capacity to stand apart from the ego and to master it. It is a memorial of the former weakness and dependence of the ego, and the mature ego remains subject to its domination. As the child was once under a compulsion to obey its parents, so the ego submits to the categorical imperative of its super-ego.

But the derivation of the super-ego from the first object-cathexes of the id, from the Oedipus complex, signifies even more for it. This derivation, as we have already shown [p. 33ff.], brings it into relation with the phylogenetic acquisitions of the id and makes it a reincarnation of former ego-structures which have left their precipitates behind in the id. Thus the super-ego is always close to the id and can act as its representative *vis-à-vis* the ego. It reaches deep down into the id and for that reason is farther from consciousness than the ego is.[1]

We shall best appreciate these relations by turning to certain clinical facts, which have long since lost their novelty but which still await theoretical discussion.

There are certain people who behave in a quite peculiar fashion during the work of analysis. When one speaks hopefully to them or expresses satisfaction with the progress of the treatment, they show signs of discontent and their condition invariably becomes worse. One begins by regarding this as defiance and as an attempt to prove their superiority to the physician, but later one comes to take a deeper and juster view. One becomes convinced, not only that such people cannot endure any praise or appreciation, but that they react inversely to the progress of the treatment. Every partial solution that ought to result, and in other people does

---

[1] It may be said that the psycho-analytic or metapsychological ego stands on its head no less than the anatomical ego—the 'cortical homunculus' [p. 20].

result, in an improvement or a temporary suspension of symptoms produces in them for the time being an exacerbation of their illness; they get worse during the treatment instead of getting better. They exhibit what is known as a 'negative therapeutic reaction'.

There is no doubt that there is something in these people that sets itself against their recovery, and its approach is dreaded as though it were a danger. We are accustomed to say that the need for illness has got the upper hand in them over the desire for recovery. If we analyse this resistance in the usual way—then, even after allowance has been made for an attitude of defiance towards the physician and for fixation to the various forms of gain from illness, the greater part of it is still left over; and this reveals itself as the most powerful of all obstacles to recovery, more powerful than the familiar ones of narcissistic inaccessibility, a negative attitude towards the physician and clinging to the gain from illness.

In the end we come to see that we are dealing with what may be called a 'moral' factor, a sense of guilt, which is finding its satisfaction in the illness and refuses to give up the punishment of suffering. We shall be right in regarding this disheartening explanation as final. But as far as the patient is concerned this sense of guilt is dumb; it does not tell him he is guilty; he does not feel guilty, he feels ill. This sense of guilt expresses itself only as a resistance to recovery which it is extremely difficult to overcome. It is also particularly difficult to convince the patient that this motive lies behind his continuing to be ill; he holds fast to the more obvious explanation that treatment by analysis is not the right remedy for his case.[2]

---

[2]The battle with the obstacle of an unconscious sense of guilt is not made easy for the analyst. Nothing can be done against it directly, and nothing

The description we have given applies to the most extreme instances of this state of affairs, but in a lesser measure this factor has to be reckoned with in very many cases, perhaps in all comparatively severe cases of neurosis. In fact it may be precisely this element in the situation, the attitude of the ego ideal, that determines the severity of a neurotic illness. We shall not hesitate, therefore, to discuss rather more fully the way in which the sense of guilt expresses itself under different conditions.

An interpretation of the normal, conscious sense of guilt (conscience) presents no difficulties; it is based on the tension between the ego and the ego ideal and is the expression of a condemnation of the ego by its critical agency. The

---

indirectly but the slow procedure of unmasking its unconscious repressed roots, and of thus gradually changing it into a *conscious* sense of guilt. One has a special opportunity for influencing it when this *Ucs.* sense of guilt is a 'borrowed' one—when it is the product of an identification with some other person who was once the object of an erotic cathexis. A sense of guilt that has been adopted in this way is often the sole remaining trace of the abandoned love-relation and not at all easy to recognize as such. (The likeness between this process and what happens in melancholia is unmistakable.) If one can unmask this former object-cathexis behind the *Ucs.* sense of guilt, the therapeutic success is often brilliant, but otherwise the outcome of one's efforts is by no means certain. It depends principally on the intensity of the sense of guilt; there is often no counteracting force of a similar order of strength which the treatment can oppose to it. Perhaps it may depend, too, on whether the personality of the analyst allows of the patient's putting him in the place of his ego ideal, and this involves a temptation for the analyst to play the part of prophet, saviour and redeemer to the patient. Since the rules of analysis are diametrically opposed to the physician's making use of his personality in any such manner, it must be honestly confessed that here we have another limitation to the effectiveness of analysis; after all, analysis does not set out to make pathological reactions impossible, but to give the patient's ego *freedom* to decide one way or the other.—[Freud returned to this topic in his paper on 'The Economic Problem of Masochism' (1924c), *S.E.*, **19**, 166, where he discussed the distinction between the unconscious sense of guilt and moral masochism. See also Chapters VII and VIII of *Civilization and its Discontents* (1930a).]

feelings of inferiority so well known in neurotics are presumably not far removed from it. In two very familiar maladies the sense of guilt is over-strongly conscious; in them the ego ideal displays particular severity and often rages against the ego in a cruel fashion. The attitude of the ego ideal in these two conditions, obsessional neurosis and melancholia, presents, alongside of this similarity, differences that are no less significant.

In certain forms of obsessional neurosis the sense of guilt is over-noisy but cannot justify itself to the ego. Consequently the patient's ego rebels against the imputation of guilt and seeks the physician's support in repudiating it. It would be folly to acquiesce in this, for to do so would have no effect. Analysis eventually shows that the super-ego is being influenced by processes that have remained unknown to the ego. It is possible to discover the repressed impulses which are really at the bottom of the sense of guilt. Thus in this case the super-ego knew more than the ego about the unconscious id.

In melancholia the impression that the super-ego has obtained a hold upon consciousness is even stronger. But here the ego ventures no objection; it admits its guilt and submits to the punishment. We understand the difference. In obsessional neurosis what were in question were objectionable impulses which remained outside the ego, while in melancholia the object to which the super-ego's wrath applies has been taken into the ego through identification.

It is certainly not clear why the sense of guilt reaches such an extraordinary strength in these two neurotic disorders; but the main problem presented in this state of affairs lies in another direction. We shall postpone discussion of it until we have dealt with the other cases in which the sense of guilt remains unconscious. [See p. 54.]

It is essentially in hysteria and in states of a hysterical type that this is found. Here the mechanism by which the sense of guilt remains unconscious is easy to discover. The hysterical ego fends off a distressing perception with which the criticisms of its super-ego threaten it, in the same way in which it is in the habit of fending off an unendurable object-cathexis—by an act of repression. It is the ego, therefore, that is responsible for the sense of guilt remaining unconscious. We know that as a rule the ego carries out repressions in the service and at the behest of its super-ego; but this is a case in which it has turned the same weapon against its harsh taskmaster. In obsessional neurosis, as we know, the phenomena of reaction-formation predominate; but here [in hysteria] the ego succeeds only in keeping at a distance the material to which the sense of guilt refers.

One may go further and venture the hypothesis that a great part of the sense of guilt must normally remain unconscious, because the origin of conscience is intimately connected with the Oedipus complex, which belongs to the unconscious. If anyone were inclined to put forward the paradoxical proposition that the normal man is not only far more immoral than he believes but also far more moral than he knows, psycho-analysis, on whose findings the first half of the assertion rests, would have no objection to raise against the second half.[3]

It was a surprise to find that an increase in this *Ucs.* sense of guilt can turn people into criminals. But it is undoubtedly a fact. In many criminals, especially youthful ones, it is possible to detect a very powerful sense of guilt which existed before the crime, and is therefore not its result but its motive. It is as if it was a relief to be able to fasten this

---

[3]This proposition is only apparently a paradox; it simply states that human nature has a far greater extent, both for good and for evil, than it thinks it has—i.e. than its ego is aware of through conscious perception.

unconscious sense of guilt on to something real and immediate.[4]

In all these situations the super-ego displays its independence of the conscious ego and its intimate relations with the unconscious id. Having regard, now, to the importance we have ascribed to preconscious verbal residues in the ego [p. 12 f.], the question arises whether it can be the case that the super-ego, in so far as it is *Ucs.*, consists in such word-presentations and, if it does not, what else it consists in. Our tentative answer will be that it is as impossible for the super-ego as for the ego to disclaim its origin from things heard; for it is a part of the ego and remains accessible to consciousness by way of these word-presentations (concepts, abstractions). But the *cathectic energy* does not reach these contents of the super-ego from auditory perception (instruction or reading) but from sources in the id.

The question which we put off answering [see p. 52] runs as follows: How is it that the super-ego manifests itself essentially as a sense of guilt (or rather, as criticism—for the sense of guilt is the perception in the ego answering to this criticism) and moreover develops such extraordinary harshness and severity towards the ego? If we turn to melancholia first, we find that the excessively strong super-ego which has obtained a hold upon consciousness rages against the ego with merciless violence, as if it had taken possession of the whole of the sadism available in the person concerned. Following our view of sadism, we should say that the destructive component had entrenched itself in the super-ego and turned against the ego. What is now holding sway in the super-ego is, as it were, a pure culture of the death instinct,

---

[4][A full discussion of this (together with some other references) will be found in Part III of Freud's paper on 'Some Character Types' (1916*d*), *Standard Ed.*, 14, 332–3.]

and in fact it often enough succeeds in driving the ego into death, if the latter does not fend off its tyrant in time by the change round into mania.

The reproaches of conscience in certain forms of obsessional neurosis are as distressing and tormenting, but here the situation is less perspicuous. It is noteworthy that the obsessional neurotic, in contrast to the melancholic, never in fact takes the step of self-destruction; it is as though he were immune against the danger of suicide, and he is far better protected from it than the hysteric. We can see that what guarantees the safety of the ego is the fact that the object has been retained. In obsessional neurosis it has become possible, through a regression to the pregenital organization, for the love-impulses to transform themselves into impulses of aggression against the object. Here again the instinct of destruction has been set free and it seeks to destroy the object, or at least it appears to have that intention. These purposes have not been adopted by the ego and it struggles against them with reaction-formations and precautionary measures; they remain in the id. The superego, however, behaves as if the ego were responsible for them and shows at the same time by the seriousness with which it chastises these destructive intentions that they are no mere semblance evoked by regression but an actual substitution of hate for love. Helpless in both directions, the ego defends itself vainly, alike against the instigations of the murderous id and against the reproaches of the punishing conscience. It succeeds in holding in check at least the most brutal actions of both sides; the first outcome is interminable self-torment, and eventually there follows a systematic torturing of the object, in so far as it is within reach.

The dangerous death instincts are dealt with in the individual in various ways: in part they are rendered harmless by being fused with erotic components, in part they are diverted towards the external world in the form of aggression, while to a large extent they undoubtedly continue their internal work unhindered. How is it then that in melancholia the super-ego can become a kind of gathering-place for the death instincts?

From the point of view of instinctual control, of morality, it may be said of the id that it is totally non-moral, of the ego that it strives to be moral, and of the super-ego that it can be super-moral and then become as cruel as only the id can be. It is remarkable that the more a man checks his aggressiveness towards the exterior the more severe—that is aggressive—he becomes in his ego ideal. The ordinary view sees the situation the other way round: the standard set up by the ego ideal seems to be the motive for the suppression of aggressiveness. The fact remains, however, as we have stated it: the more a man controls his aggressiveness, the more intense becomes his ideal's inclination to aggressiveness against his ego.[5] It is like a displacement, a turning round upon his own ego. But even ordinary normal morality has a harshly restraining, cruelly prohibiting quality. It is from this, indeed, that the conception arises of a higher being who deals out punishment inexorably.

I cannot go further in my consideration of these questions without introducing a fresh hypothesis. The super-ego arises, as we know, from an identification with the father taken as a model. Every such identification is in the nature of a desexualization or even of a sublimation. It now seems as though when a transformation of this kind takes place, an instinctual defusion occurs at the same time [p. 25]. After sublimation the erotic component no longer has the power

---

[5][Freud returned to this paradox in Section B of 'Some Additional Notes on Dream-Interpretation as a Whole' (1925*i*), *S.E.*, 19, 134, and also in 'The Economic Problem of Masochism' (1924*c*), ibid., 170, and discussed it more fully in Chapter VII of *Civilization and its Discontents* (1930*a*).]

to bind the whole of the destructiveness that was combined with it, and this is released in the form of an inclination to aggression and destruction. This defusion would be the source of the general character of harshness and cruelty exhibited by the ideal—its dictatorial 'Thou shalt'.

Let us again consider obsessional neurosis for a moment. The state of affairs is different here. The defusion of love into aggressiveness has not been effected by the work of the ego, but is the result of a regression which has come about in the id. But this process has extended beyond the id to the super-ego, which now increases its severity towards the innocent ego. It would seem, however, that in this case, no less than in that of melancholia, the ego, having gained control over the libido by means of identification, is punished for doing so by the super-ego through the instrumentality of the aggressiveness which was mixed with the libido.

Our ideas about the ego are beginning to clear, and its various relationships are gaining distinctness. We now see the ego in its strength and in its weaknesses. It is entrusted with important functions. By virtue of its relation to the perceptual system it gives mental processes an order in time and submits them to 'reality-testing'.[6] By interposing the processes of thinking, it secures a postponement of motor discharges and controls the access to motility.[7] This last power is, to be sure, a question more of form than of fact; in the matter of action the ego's position is like that of a constitutional monarch, without whose sanction no law can be passed but who hesitates long before imposing his veto on any measure put forward by Parliament. All the experiences of life that originate from without enrich the ego; the

---

[6][Cf. 'The Unconscious' (1915e), *Standard Ed.*, 14, 188.]
[7][Cf. 'Formulations on the Two Principles of Mental Functioning' (1911b), *Standard Ed.*, 12, 221.]

id, however, is its second external world, which it strives to bring into subjection to itself. It withdraws libido from the id and transforms the object-cathexes of the id into ego-structures. With the aid of the super-ego, in a manner that is still obscure to us, it draws upon the experiences of past ages stored in the id [p. 34].

There are two paths by which the contents of the id can penetrate into the ego. The one is direct, the other leads by way of the ego ideal; which of these two paths they take may, for some mental activities, be of decisive importance: The ego develops from perceiving instincts to controlling them, from obeying instincts to inhibiting them. In this achievement a large share is taken by the ego ideal, which indeed is partly a reaction-formation against the instinctual processes of the id. Psycho-analysis is an instrument to enable the ego to achieve a progressive conquest of the id.

From the other point of view, however, we see this same ego as a poor creature owing service to three masters and consequently menaced by three dangers: from the external world, from the libido of the id, and from the severity of the super-ego. Three kinds of anxiety correspond to these three dangers, since anxiety is the expression of a retreat from danger. As a frontier-creature, the ego tries to mediate between the world and the id, to make the id pliable to the world and, by means of its muscular activity, to make the world fall in with the wishes of the id. In point of fact it behaves like the physician during an analytic treatment: it offers itself, with the attention it pays to the real world, as a libidinal object to the id, and aims at attaching the id's libido to itself. It is not only a helper to the id; it is also a submissive slave who courts his master's love. Whenever possible, it tries to remain on good terms with the id; it clothes the id's *Ucs.* commands with its *Pcs.* rationalizations; it pretends that the id is showing obedience to the admonitions of reality, even when in fact it is remaining

[margin handwritten note: How contents of the ID penetrate into the Ego.]

obstinate and unyielding; it disguises the id's conflicts with reality and, if possible, its conflicts with the super-ego too. In its position midway between the id and reality, it only too often yields to the temptation to become sycophantic, opportunist and lying, like a politician who sees the truth but wants to keep his place in popular favour.

Towards the two classes of instincts the ego's attitude is not impartial. Through its work of identification and sublimation it gives the death instincts in the id assistance in gaining control over the libido, but in so doing it runs the risk of becoming the object of the death instincts and of itself perishing. In order to be able to help in this way it has had itself to become filled with libido; it thus itself becomes the representative of Eros and thenceforward desires to live and to be loved.

But since the ego's work of sublimation results in a defusion of the instincts and a liberation of the aggressive instincts in the super-ego, its struggle against the libido exposes it to the danger of maltreatment and death. In suffering under the attacks of the super-ego or perhaps even succumbing to them, the ego is meeting with a fate like that of the protista which are destroyed by the products of decomposition that they themselves have created.[8] From the economic point of view the morality that functions in the super-ego seems to be a similar product of decomposition.

Among the dependent relationships in which the ego stands, that to the super-ego is perhaps the most interesting.

The ego is the actual seat of anxiety.[9] Threatened by dangers from three directions, it develops the flight-reflex by

---

[8][Freud had discussed these animalculae in 1920g, *Standard Ed.*, 18, 48; *I.P.L.*, 4, 42. These would probably now be described as 'protozoa' rather than 'protista'.]

[9][What follows on the subject of anxiety must be read in connection with Freud's revised views as stated in *Inhibitions, Symptoms and Anxiety* (1926d), where most of the points raised here are further discussed.]

withdrawing its own cathexis from the menacing perception
or from the similarly regarded process in the id, and emitting
it as anxiety. This primitive reaction is later replaced by the
carrying-out of protective cathexes (the mechanism of the
phobias). What it is that the ego fears from the external and
from the libidinal danger cannot be specified; we know that
the fear is of being overwhelmed or annihilated, but it cannot be grasped analytically.[10] The ego is simply obeying the
warning of the pleasure principle. On the other hand, we
can tell what is hidden behind the ego's dread of the super-
ego, the fear of conscience.[11] The superior being, which
turned into the ego ideal, once threatened castration, and
this dread of castration is probably the nucleus round which
the subsequent fear of conscience has gathered; it is this
dread that persists as the fear of conscience.

The high-sounding phrase, 'every fear is ultimately the
fear of death', has hardly any meaning, and at any rate
cannot be justified.[12] It seems to me, on the contrary, perfectly correct to distinguish the fear of death from dread of
an object (realistic anxiety) and from neurotic libidinal anxiety. It presents a difficult problem to psycho-analysis, for
death is an abstract concept with a negative content for
which no unconscious correlative can be found. It would
seem that the mechanism of the fear of death can only be

---

[10][The notion of the ego being 'overwhelmed' (of an '*Überwältigung*')
occurs very early in Freud's writings. See, for instance, a mention of it in
Part II of his first paper on 'The Neuro-Psychoses of Defence' (1894*a*). But
it plays a prominent part in his discussion of the mechanism of the neuroses
in Draft K of January 1, 1896, in the Fliess correspondence (Freud, 1950*a*).
There is an evident connection here with the 'traumatic situation' of
Inhibitions, Symptoms and Anxiety (1926*d*).]

[11]['*Gewissensangst.*' An Editor's footnote on the use of this word will be
found in Chapter VII of *Inhibitions, Symptoms and Anxiety, Standard Ed.*,
20, 128; *I.P.L.*, 28, 42.]

[12][Cf. Stekel (1908, 5).]

that the ego relinquishes its narcissistic libidinal cathexis in a very large measure—that is, that it gives up itself, just as it gives up some *external* object in other cases in which it feels anxiety. I believe that the fear of death is something that occurs between the ego and the super-ego.

We know that the fear of death makes its appearance under two conditions (which, moreover, are entirely analogous to situations in which other kinds of anxiety develop), namely, as a reaction to an external danger and as an internal process, as for instance in melancholia. Once again a neurotic manifestation may help us to understand a normal one.

The fear of death in melancholia only admits of one explanation: that the ego gives itself up because it feels itself hated and persecuted by the super-ego, instead of loved. To the ego, therefore, living means the same as being loved— being loved by the super-ego, which here again appears as the representative of the id. The super-ego fulfils the same function of protecting and saving that was fulfilled in earlier days by the father and later by Providence or Destiny. But, when the ego finds itself in an excessive real danger which it believes itself unable to overcome by its own strength, it is bound to draw the same conclusion. It sees itself deserted by all protecting forces and lets itself die. Here, moreover, is once again the same situation as that which underlay the first great anxiety-state of birth[13] and the infantile anxiety of longing—the anxiety due to separation from the protecting mother.[14]

These considerations make it possible to regard the fear of death, like the fear of conscience, as a development of the

---

[13][Some discussion of the appearance of this notion here will be found in the Editor's Introduction to *Inhibitions, Symptoms and Anxiety, Standard Ed.*, 20, 85–6; *I.P.L.*, 28, xvii–xviii.]

[14][This foreshadows the 'separation anxiety' discussed in *Inhibitions, Symptoms and Anxiety* (1926d), *Standard Ed.*, 20, 151; *I.P.L.*, 28, 65.]

fear of castration. The great significance which the sense of guilt has in the neuroses makes it conceivable that common neurotic anxiety is reinforced in severe cases by the generating of anxiety between the ego and the super-ego (fear of castration, of conscience, of death).

The id, to which we finally come back, has no means of showing the ego either love or hate. It cannot say what it wants; it has achieved no unified will. Eros and the death instinct struggle within it; we have seen with what weapons the one group of instincts defends itself against the other. It would be possible to picture the id as under the domination of the mute but powerful death instincts, which desire to be at peace and (prompted by the pleasure principle) to put Eros, the mischiefmaker, to rest; but perhaps that might be to undervalue the part played by Eros.

APPENDIX A

The Descriptive and the Dynamic Unconscious

A curious point arises out of two sentences which appear on pp. 5 and 6 above. The Editor's attention was drawn to it in a private communication from Dr. Ernest Jones, who had come across it in the course of examining Freud's correspondence.

On October 28, 1923, a few months after this work appeared, Ferenczi wrote to Freud in these terms: '... Nevertheless I venture to put a question to you .... since there is a passage in *The Ego and the Id* which, without your solution, I do not understand. ... On p. 13[1] I find the following: "... that in the descriptive sense there are two kinds of unconscious, but in the dynamic sense only one." Since, however, you write on p. 12[1] that the latent unconscious is unconscious only descriptively, not in the dynamic sense, I had thought that it was precisely the dynamic line of approach that called for the hypothesis of there being two sorts of *Ucs.*, while description knows only *Cs.* and *Ucs.*'

To this Freud replied on October 30, 1923: '... Your question about the passage on p. 13 of *The Ego and the Id* has positively horrified me. What appears there gives a directly opposite sense to p. 12; and in the sentence on p. 13

---

[1]Of the German edition. Sentences are on pp. 5 and 6 here.

"descriptive" and "dynamic" have simply been transposed.'

A little consideration of this startling affair suggests, how-ever, that Ferenczi's criticism was based on a misunder-standing and that Freud was over-hasty in accepting it. The confusions which underlie Ferenczi's remarks are not very easily sorted out, and a rather lengthy argument is inevita-ble. Since, however, others besides Ferenczi may fall into the same error, it seems worth while to try to clear the matter up.

We will start off with the first half of Freud's later sen-tence: 'in the descriptive sense there are two kinds of uncon-scious.' The meaning of this seems perfectly clear: the term 'unconscious' in its descriptive sense covers two things—the latent unconscious and the repressed unconscious. Freud might, however, have expressed the idea even more clearly. Instead of 'two kinds of unconscious [*zweierlei Un-bewusstes*]' he might have said explicitly that in the descrip-tive sense there are 'two kinds of things that are uncon-scious'. And in fact Ferenczi evidently misunderstood the words: he took them to be saying that the term 'descriptively unconscious' had two different *meanings*. This, as he rightly saw, could not be so: the term unconscious, used descrip-tively, could only have one meaning—that the thing it was applied to was not conscious. In logical terminology, he thought Freud was speaking of the *connotation* of the term whereas he was actually speaking of its *denotation*.

We now proceed to the second half of Freud's later sentence: 'but in the dynamic sense [there is] only one [kind of unconscious]'. Here again the meaning seems perfectly clear: the term 'unconscious' in its dynamic sense covers only one thing—the repressed unconscious. This is once more a statement about the *denotation* of the term; though even if it had been about its *connotation* it would still be true—the term 'dynamic unconscious' can only have one meaning. Ferenczi, however, objects to it, on the ground that 'it was precisely the dynamic line of approach that called for the hypothesis of there being two sorts of *Ucs.*'. Ferenczi was once more misunderstanding Freud. He took him to be saying that if we consider the term 'unconscious', bearing dynamic factors in mind, we see that it has only one meaning—which would, of course, have been the opposite of everything that Freud was arguing. Whereas what Freud really meant was that all the things that are unconscious dynamically (i.e. that are repressed) fall into one class.—The position is made a little more confused by Ferenczi's using the symbol '*Ucs.*' to mean 'unconscious' in the descriptive sense—a slip which Freud himself makes by implication on p. 9.

Thus this later sentence of Freud's seems altogether immune from criticism in itself. But is it, as Ferenczi suggests and as Freud himself seems to agree, incompatible with the earlier sentence? This earlier sentence speaks of the latent unconscious as being 'unconscious only descriptively, not in the dynamic sense'. Ferenczi appears to have thought that this contradicts the later statement that 'in the descriptive sense there are two kinds of unconscious'. But the two statements do not contradict each other: the fact that the latent unconscious is only descriptively unconscious does not in the least imply that it is the only thing that is descriptively unconscious.

There is, indeed, a passage in Lecture XXXI of Freud's *New Introductory Lectures,* written some ten years later than the present work, in which the whole of this argument is repeated in very similar terms. In that passage it is explained more than once that in the descriptive sense both the preconscious and the repressed are unconscious, but that in the dynamic sense the term is restricted to the repressed.

It must be pointed out that this interchange of letters

took place only a very few days after Freud had undergone an extremely severe operation. He was not yet able to write (his reply was dictated), and he was probably in no condition to weigh the argument thoroughly. It seems likely that on reflection he realized that Ferenczi's discovery was a mare's nest, for the passage was never altered in the later editions of the book.

APPENDIX B

The Great Reservoir of Libido

There is considerable difficulty over this matter, which is mentioned in the first footnote on p. 25 and discussed at greater length on p. 45.

The analogy seems to have made its first appearance in a new section added to the third edition of the *Three Essays* (1905*d*), which was published in 1915 but had been prepared by Freud in the autumn of 1914. The passage runs (*S.E.*, 7, 218; *I.P.L.*, 57, 84): 'Narcissistic or ego libido seems to be the great reservoir from which the object-cathexes are sent out and into which they are withdrawn once more; the narcissistic libidinal cathexis of the ego is the original state of things, realized in earliest childhood, and is merely covered by the later extrusions of libido, but in essentials persists behind them.'

The same notion had, however, been expressed earlier in another favourite analogy of Freud's, which appears sometimes as an alternative and sometimes alongside the 'great reservoir'.[1] This earlier passage is in the paper on narcissism itself (1914*c*), which was written by Freud in the early part

---

[1] This analogy had appeared already in a rudimentary form in the third essay in *Totem and Taboo*, which was first published early in 1913. (*Standard Ed.*, 13, 89.)

of the same year, 1914 (*Standard Ed.*, **14,** 75): 'Thus we form the idea of there being an original libidinal cathexis of the ego, from which some is later given off to objects, but which fundamentally persists and is related to the object-cathexis much as the body of an amoeba is related to the pseudopodia which it puts out.'

The two analogies appear together in a semi-popular paper written at the end of 1916 for a Hungarian periodical ('A Difficulty in the Path of Psycho-Analysis', 1917*a*, *Standard Ed.*, **17,** 139): 'The ego is a great reservoir from which the libido that is destined for objects flows out and into which it flows back from those objects . . . As an illustration of this state of things we may think of an amoeba, whose viscous substance puts out pseudopodia . . .'

The amoeba appears once more in Lecture XXVI of the *Introductory Lectures* (1916–17), dating from 1917, and the reservoir in *Beyond the Pleasure Principle* (1920*g*), *S.E.*, **18,** 51; *I.P.L.*, **4,** 45: 'Psycho-analysis . . . came to the conclusion that the ego is the true and original reservoir of libido, and that it is only from that reservoir that libido is extended on to objects.'

Freud included a very similar passage in an encyclopaedia article which he wrote in the summer of 1922 (1923*a*, *Standard Ed.*, **18,** 257), and then almost immediately afterwards came the announcement of the id, and what appears like a drastic correction of the earlier statements: 'Now that we have distinguished between the ego and the id, we must recognize the id as the great reservoir of libido . . .' And again: 'At the very beginning, all the libido is accumulated in the id, while the ego is still in process of formation or is still feeble. The id sends part of this libido out into erotic object-cathexes, whereupon the ego, now grown stronger, tries to get hold of this object-libido and to force itself on the id as a love-object. The narcissism of the ego is thus a

secondary one, which has been withdrawn from objects.'
(Pp. 25n. and 45 above.)

This new position seems quite clearly intelligible, and it
is therefore a little disturbing to come upon the following
sentence, written only a year or so after *The Ego and the Id,*
in the *Autobiographical Study* (1925d [1924]), *Standard
Ed.,* 20, 56: 'All through the subject's life his ego remains
the great reservoir of his libido, from which object cathexes
are sent out and into which the libido can stream back again
from the objects.'[2]

The sentence, it is true, occurs in the course of a historical
sketch of the development of psycho-analytic theory; but
there is no indication of the change of view announced in
The Ego and the Id. And, finally, we find this passage in one
of Freud's very last writings, in Chapter II of the *Outline
of Psycho-Analysis* (1940a), written in 1938: 'It is hard to
say anything of the behaviour of the libido in the id and in
the super-ego. All that we know about it relates to the ego,
in which at first the whole available quota of libido is stored
up. We call this state the absolutely primary narcissism. It
lasts till the ego begins to cathect the ideas of objects with
libido, to transform narcissistic libido into object-libido.
Throughout the whole of life the ego remains the great
reservoir, from which libidinal cathexes are sent out to objects and into which they are also once more withdrawn, just
as an amoeba behaves with its pseudopodia.'

Do these later passages imply that Freud had retracted
the opinions he expressed in the present work? It seems
difficult to believe it, and there are two points that may help
towards a reconciliation of the apparently conflicting views.
The first is a very small one. The analogy of the 'reservoir'

---

[2]An almost identical statement is made in Lecture XXXII of the *New
Introductory Lectures* (1933a).

is from its very nature an ambiguous one: a reservoir can be regarded either as a water storage tank or as a source of water supply. There is no great difficulty in applying the image in both senses both to the ego and to the id, and it would certainly have clarified the various passages that have been quoted—and in particular the footnote on p. 25—if Freud had shown more precisely which picture was in his mind.

The second point is of greater importance. In the *New Introductory Lectures,* only a few pages after the passage referred to in the footnote above, in the course of a discussion of masochism, Freud writes: 'If it is true of the destructive instinct as well that the ego—but what we have in mind here is rather the id, the whole person—originally includes all the instinctual impulses . . .' The parenthesis points, of course, to a primitive state of things in which the id and the ego are still undifferentiated.[3] And there is a similar, but more definite, remark in the *Outline,* this time two paragraphs before the passage already quoted: 'We picture some such initial state as one in which the total available energy of Eros, which henceforward we shall speak of as "libido", is present in the still undifferentiated ego-id . . .' If we take this as being the true essence of Freud's theory, the apparent contradiction in his expression of it is diminished. This 'ego-id' was originally the 'great reservoir of libido' in the sense of being a storage tank. After differentiation had occurred, the id would continue as a storage tank but, when it began sending out cathexes (whether to objects or to the now differentiated ego) it would in addition be a source of supply. But the same would be true of the ego as well, for it would be a storage tank of narcissistic libido as well as, on one view, a source of supply for object-cathexes.

This last point leads us, however, to a further question,

---

[3]This is, of course, a familiar view of Freud's.

on which it seems inevitable to suppose that Freud held different views at different times. In *The Ego and the Id* (p. 45) 'at the very beginning, all the libido is accumulated in the id'; then 'the id sends part of this libido out into erotic object-cathexes', which the ego tries to get control of by forcing itself on the id as a love-object: 'the narcissism of the ego is thus a secondary one.' But in the *Outline*, 'at first the whole available quota of libido is stored up in the ego', 'we call this state the absolutely primary narcissism' and 'it lasts until the ego begins to cathect the ideas of objects with libido'. Two different processes seem to be envisaged in these two accounts. In the first the original object-cathexes are thought of as going out direct from the id, and only reaching the ego indirectly; in the second the whole of the libido is thought of as going from the id to the ego and only reaching the objects indirectly. The two processes do not seem incompatible, and it is possible that both may occur; but on this question Freud is silent.

LIST OF ABBREVIATIONS

G.S. = Freud, *Gesammelte Schriften* (12 vols.), Vienna, 1924–34

G.W. = Freud, *Gesammelte Werke* (18 vols.), London from 1940

C.P. = Freud, *Collected Papers* (5 vols.), London, 1924–50

S.E.
Standard Ed. } = Freud, *Standard Edition* (24 vols.), London, from 1953

I.P.L. International Psycho-Analytical Library, Hogarth Press and Institute of Psycho-Analysis, London, from 1921

Theoretische Schriften = Freud, *Theoretische Schriften* (1911–25), Vienna, 1931

BIBLIOGRAPHY
& AUTHOR INDEX

[Titles of books and periodicals are in italics; titles of papers are in inverted commas. Abbreviations are in accordance with the *World List of Scientific Periodicals* (London, 1952). Further abbreviations used in this volume will be found in the List on page 73. Numerals in thick type refer to volumes; ordinary numerals refer to pages. The figures in round brackets at the end of each entry indicate the page or pages of this volume on which the work in question is mentioned. In the case of the Freud entries, the letters attached to the dates of publication are in accordance with the corresponding entries in the complete bibliography of Freud's writings to be included in the last volume of the *Standard Edition*.

For non-technical authors, and for technical authors where no specific work is mentioned, see the General Index.]

BREUER, J., and FREUD, S. (1895). See FREUD, S., (1895*d*)

FERENCZI, S. (1913) 'Entwicklungsstufen des Wirklichkeitssinnes', *Int. Z. (ärztl.) Psychoanal.*, **1**, 124. (31)
    [*Trans.:* 'Stages in the Development of the Sense of Reality', *First Contributions to Psycho-Analysis*, London, 1952, Chap. VIII.]

FREUD, S. (1891*b*) *Zur Auffassung der Aphasien*, Vienna. (13)
    [*Trans.: On Aphasia*, London and New York, 1953.]

    (1894*a*) 'Die Abwehr-Neuropsychosen', *G.S.*, **1**, 290; *G. W.*, **1**, 59. (21, 60).
    [*Trans.:* 'The Neuro-Psychoses of Defence' *C.P.*, **1**, 59; *Standard Ed.*, **3**, 43.]

    (1895*d*) With BREUER, J., *Studien über Hysterie*, Vienna. *G.S.*, **1**, 3; *G. W.*, **1**, 77 (omitting Breuer's contributions). (xxx, 13)
    [*Trans.: Studies on Hysteria*, *Standard Ed.*, **2**; *I.P.L.*, 50. Including Breuer's contributions.]

(1896*b*) 'Weitere Bemerkungen über die Abwehr-Neuropsychosen', *G.S.*, 1, 363; *G.W.*, 1, 379. (xxxii, 9)

[*Trans.:* 'Further Remarks on the Neuro-Psychoses of Defence', *C.P.*, 1, 155; *Standard Ed.*, 3, 159.]

(1900*a*) *Die Traumdeutung*, Vienna. *G.S.*, 2–3; *G.W.*, 2–3. (xxix–xxx, 18, 19, 21)

[*Trans.: The Interpretation of Dreams*, London and New York, 1955; *Standard Ed.*, 4–5.]

(1905*c*) *Der Witz und seine Beziehung zum Unbewussten*, Vienna. *G.S.*, 9, 5; *G.W.*, 6. (44)

[*Trans.: Jokes and their Relation to the Unconscious*, London, 1960; *Standard Ed.*, 8.]

(1905*d*) *Drei Abhandlungen zur Sexualtheorie*, Vienna. *G.S.*, 5, 3; *G.W.*, 5, 29. (29, 46, 67)

[*Trans.: Three Essays on the Theory of Sexuality, Standard Ed.*, 7, 125; *I.P.L.*, 57.]

(1907*b*) 'Zwangshandlungen und Religionsübung', *G.S.*, 10, 210; *G.W.*, 7, 129. (xxxv, 21)

[*Trans.:* 'Obsessive Actions and Religious Practices', *C.P.*, 2, 25; *Standard Ed.*, 9, 116.]

(1908*b*) 'Charakter und Analerotik', *G.S.*, 5, 261; *G.W.*, 7, 203. (23).

[*Trans.:* 'Character and Anal Erotism', *C.P.*, 2, 45; *Standard Ed.*, 9, 169.]

(1910*c*) *Eine Kindheitserinnerung des Leonardo da Vinci*, Vienna. *G.S.*, 9, 371; *G.W.*, 8, 128. (xxxiv, xxxvi)

[*Trans.: Leonardo da Vinci and a Memory of His Childhood, Standard Ed.*, 11, 59.]

(1910*i*) 'Die psychogene Sehstörung in psychoanalytischer Auffassung', *G.S.*, 5, 310; *G.W.*, 8, 94. (xxxiv)

[*Trans.:* 'The Psycho-Analytic View of Psychogenic Disturbance of Vision', *C.P.*, 2, 105; *Standard Ed.*, 11, 211.]

(1911*b*) 'Formulierungen über die zwei Prinzipien des psychischen Geschehens', *G.S.*, 5, 409; *G.W.*, 8, 230. (xxxiv, 57)

[*Trans.:* 'Formulations on the Two Principles of Mental Functioning', *C.P.*, 4, 13; *Standard Ed.*, 12, 215.]

(1911*c*) 'Psychoanalytische Bemerkungen über einen autobiographisch beschriebenen Fall von Paranoia (Dementia Paranoides)', *G.S.*, 8, 355; *G.W.*, 8, 240. (xxxiv)

[*Trans.:* 'Psycho-Analytic Notes on an Autobiographical Account of a Case of Paranoia (Dementia Paranoides)', *C.P.*, 3, 387; *Standard Ed.*, 11, 3.]

(1912g) 'A Note on the Unconscious in Psycho-Analysis' [in English], *C.P.*, 4, 22; *Standard Ed.*, 12, 257. (xxx, xxxi, 5, 7)

[*German Trans.* (by Hanns Sachs): 'Einige Bemerkungen über den Begriff des Unbewussten in der Psychoanalyse', *G.S.*, 5, 433; *G.W.*, 8, 430.]

(1912–13) *Totem und Tabu*, Vienna, 1913. *G.S.*, 10, 3; *G.W.*, 9. (23, 34, 67)

[*Trans.*: *Totem and Taboo*, London, 1950; New York, 1952; *Standard Ed.*, 13, 1.]

(1914c) 'Zur Einführung des Narzissmus', *G.S.*, 6, 155; *G.W.*, 10, 138. (xxxiv, xxxv, 22, 25, 27, 67).

[*Trans.*: 'On Narcissism: an Introduction', *C.P.*, 4, 30; *Standard Ed.*, 14, 69.]

(1915c) 'Triebe und Triebschicksale', *G.S.*, 5, 443; *G.W.*, 10, 210. (40, 45)

[*Trans.*: 'Instincts and their Vicissitudes', *C.P.*, 4, 60; *Standard Ed.*, 14, 111.]

(1915e) 'Das Unbewusste', *G.S.*, 5, 480; *G.W.*, 10, 264. (xxxi, xxxiv, 4, 7, 9, 12, 13, 16, 57)

[*Trans.*: 'The Unconscious', *C.P.*, 4, 98; *Standard Ed.*, 14, 161.]

(1916d) 'Einige Charaktertypen aus der psychoanalytischen Arbeit', *G.S.*, 10, 287; *G.W.*, 10, 364 (54)

[*Trans.*: 'Some Character-Types Met with in Psycho-Analytic Work', *C.P.*, 4, 318; *Standard Ed.*, 14, 311.]

(1916–17) *Vorlesungen zur Einführung in die Psychoanalyse*, Vienna. *G.S.*, 7; *G.W.*, 11. (68)

[*Trans.*: *Introductory Lectures on Psycho-Analysis*, revised ed., London, 1929 (*A General Introduction to Psychoanalysis*, New York, 1935); *Standard Ed.*, 15–16.]

(1917a) 'Eine Schwierigkeit der Psychoanalyse', *G.S.*, 10, 347; *G.W.*, 12, 3. (68)

[*Trans.*: 'A Difficulty in the Path of Psycho-Analysis', *C.P.*, 4, 347; *Standard Ed.*, 17, 137.]

(1917d) 'Metapsychologische Ergänzung zur Traumlehre', *G.S.*, 5, 520; *G.W.*, 10, 412. (22)

[*Trans.*: 'A Metapsychological Supplement to the Theory of Dreams', *C.P.*, 4, 137; *Standard Ed.*, 14, 219.]

(1917*e* [1915]) 'Trauer und Melancholie', *G.S.*, 5, 535 *G. W.*, 10, 428. (xxxv, xxxvi, 23)

[*Trans.:* 'Mourning and Melancholia', *C.P.*, 4, 152; *Standard Ed.*, 14, 239.]

(1920*g*) *Jenseits des Lustprinzips*, Vienna. *G.S.*, 6, 191; *G. W.*, 13, 3. (xxxi, xxxix, 9, 11, 15, 22, 37, 39, 45, 46, 59, 68)

[*Trans.: Beyond the Pleasure Principle, Standard Ed.*, 18, 3; *I.P.L.*, 4.]

(1921*b*) Introduction [in English] to J. Varendonck's *The Psychology of Day-Dreams*, London; *Standard Ed.*, 18, 271. (14)

[*German Text* (part only): *G.S.*, 11, 264; *G. W.*, 13, 439.]

(1921*c*) *Massenpsychologie und Ich-Analyse*, Vienna. *G.S.*, 6, 261; *G. W.*, 13, 73. (xxxv–xxxvi, 22, 23, 26, 27, 34)

[*Trans.: Group Psychology and the Analysis of the Ego, Standard Ed.*, 18, 67; *I.P.L.*, 6.]

(1922*b*) 'Über einige neurotische Mechanismen bei Eifersucht, Paranoia und Homosexualität', *G.S.*, 5, 387; *G. W.*, 13, 195. (34).

[*Trans.:* 'Some Neurotic Mechanisms in Jealousy, Paranoia and Homosexuality', *C.P.*, 2, 232; *Standard Ed.*, 18, 223.]

(1922*f*) 'Etwas vom Unbewussten' (Author's Abstract of Congress Address), *Int. Z. Psychoan.*, 8, 486.

[*Trans.:* 'Some Remarks on the Unconscious', Included in 1923*b*, *Standard Ed.*, 19, 3; *I.P.L.*, 12, ix.]

(1923*a*) ' "Psychoanalyse" und "Libido Theorie" ', *G.S.*, 11, 201, *G. W.*, 13, 211. (25, 68)

[*Trans.:* 'Two Encyclopaedia Articles', *C.P.*, 5, 107; *Standard Ed.*, 18, 235.]

(1923*b*) *Das Ich und das Es*, Vienna. *G.S.*, 6, 353; *G. W.*, 13, 237;

[*Trans.: The Ego and the Id*, London, 1927; *Standard Ed.*, 19, 3. *I.P.L.*, 12.]

(1923*e*) 'Die infantile Genitalorganisation', *G.S.*, 5, 232; *G. W.*, 13, 293. (26)

[*Trans.:* 'The Infantile Genital Organization,' *C.P.*, 2, 244; *Standard Ed.*, 19, 141.]

(1924*b*) [1923] 'Neurose und Psychose', *G.S.*, 5, 418; *G. W.*, 13, 387. (xxxvii)

[*Trans.:* 'Neurosis and Psychosis', *C.P.*, 2, 250; *Standard Ed.*, 19, 149.]

(1924*c*) 'Das ökonomische Problem des Masochismus', *G.S.*, 5, 374; *G. W.*, 13, 371. (xxxvii, 39, 51, 56)

[*Trans.:* 'The Economic Problem of Masochism', *C.P.*, 2, 255; *Standard Ed.*, 19, 157.]

(1924*d*) 'Der Untergang des Ödipuskomplexes', *G.S.*, 5, 423; *G.W.*, 13, 395. (xxxvii, 27)

[*Trans.:* 'The Dissolution of the Oedipus Complex', *C.P.*, 2, 269; *Standard Ed.*, 19, 173.]

(1924*e*) 'Die Realitätsverlust bein Neurose und Psychose', *G.S.*, 6, 409; *G.W.*, 13, 363. (xxxvii)

[*Trans.:* 'The Loss of Reality in Neurosis and Psychosis', *C.P.*, 2, 277; *Standard Ed.*, 19, 183.]

(1925*d*) [1924]) *Selbstdarstellung*, Vienna, 1934. *G.S.*, 11, 119; *G.W.*, 14, 33. (69)

[*Trans.:* An *Autobiographical Study*, London, 1935 (*Autobiography*, New York, 1935); *Standard Ed.*, 20, 3.]

(1925*i*) 'Einige Nachträge zum Ganzen der Traumdeutung', *G.S.*, 3, 172; *G.W.*, 1, 561. (xxxiii, 56)

[*Trans.:* 'Some Additional Notes upon Dream-Interpretation as a Whole', *C.P.*, 5, 150; *Standard Ed.*, 19, 125.]

(1925*j*) 'Einige psychische Folgen des anatomischen Geschlechtsunterschieds', *G.S.*, 11, 8; *G.W.*, 14, 19. (xxxvii, 27)

[*Trans.:* 'Some Psychical Consequences of the Anatomical Distinction between the Sexes', *C.P.*, 5, 186; *Standard Ed.*, 19, 243.]

(1926*d*) *Hemmung, Symptom und Angst*, Vienna. *G.S.*, 11, 23; *G.W.*, 14, 113. (xxxvii, 31, 40, 60, 61)

[*Trans.:* *Inhibitions, Symptoms and Anxiety*, *Standard Ed.*, 20, 77; *I.P.L.*, 28.]

(1926*e*) *Die Frage der Lainanalyse*, Vienna. *G.S.*, 11, 307; *G.W.*, 14, 209. (4)

[*Trans.:* *The Question of Lay Analysis*, London, 1947; *Standard Ed.*, 20, 179.]

(1927*d*) 'Der Humor', *G.S.*, 11, 402; *G.W.*, 14, 383. (22)

[*Trans.:* 'Humour', *C.P.*, 5, 215; *Standard Ed.*, 21, 161.]

(1928*b*) 'Dostojewski und die Vatertötung', *G.S.*, 12, 7; *G.W.*, 14, 399. (39)

[*Trans.:* Dostoevsky and Parricide', *C.P.*, 5, 222; *Standard Ed.*, 21, 175.]

(1930*a*) *Das Unbehagen in der Kultur*, Vienna. *G.S.*, 12, 29; *G.W.*, 14, 421. (xxxiii, xxxvii, 40, 51, 56)

[*Trans.:* *Civilization and its Discontents*, London 1930; *New York*, 1961; *Standard Ed.*, 21, 59.]

(1933*a*) *Neue Folge der Vorlesungen zur Einführung in die Psychoanalyse*, Vienna. *G.S.*, 12, 151; *G.W.*, 15, 207. (xxxi, xxxvi, 18, 33, 65, 69, 70)

   [*Trans.: New Introductory Lectures on Psycho-Analysis*, London and New York, 1933; *Standard Ed.*, 22.]

(1939*a*) [1937–39]) *Der Mann Moses und die monotheistische Religion*, *G.W.*, 16, 103. (xxxiii)

   [*Trans.: Moses and Monotheism*, London and New York, 1939; *Standard Ed.*, 23.]

(1940*a* [1938]] *Abriss der Psychoanalyse*, *G.W.*, 17, 67. (69)

   [*Trans.: An Outline of Psycho-Analysis*, London and New York, 1949; *Standard Ed.*, 23.]

(1950*a* [1887–1902]) *Aus den Anfängen der Psychoanalyse*, London. Includes 'Entwurf einer Psychologie' (1895). (xxix, xxxiii, 18, 29, 60)

   [*Trans.: The Origins of Psycho-Analysis*, London and New York, 1954. (Partly, including 'A Project for a Scientific Psychology', in *Standard Ed.*, 1.)]

GRODDECK, G. (1923) *Das Buch vom Es*, Vienna. (17)

JONES, E. (1957) *Sigmund Freud: Life and Work*, Vol. 3, London and New York. (Page references are to the English edition.) (xxvii, xxxvi)

MÜNSTERBERG, H. (1908) *Philosophie der Werte; Grundzüge einer Weltanschauung*, Leipzig. (xxxvi)

RANK, O. (1913) 'Der "Familienroman" in der Psychologie des Attentäters', *Int. Z. (ärztl.) Psychoanal.*, 1, 565. (44)

RICKMAN, J. (ed.) (1937) *General Selection from the Works of Sigmund Freud*, London. (xxxvii)

STEKEL, W. (1908) *Nervöse Angstzustände und ihre Behandlung*, Vienna. (60)

VARENDONCK, J. (1921) *The Psychology of Day-Dreams*, London. (14)

INDEX

This index includes the names of non-technical authors. It also includes the names of technical authors where no reference is made in the text to specific works. For references to specific technical works, the Bibliography should be consulted.